T0352103

SPLITTING CANE
Conversations with Bamboo Rodmakers

Ed Engle

STACKPOLE
BOOKS

Published by
STACKPOLE BOOKS
4501 Forbes Boulevard, Suite 200
Lanham, Maryland 20706
www.stackpolebooks.com

First Edition

Cover photos by Ed Engle
Cover Design by Caroline Stover with assistance from Jana Rush

Library of Congress Cataloging-in-Publication Data

Engle, Ed, 1950-
    Splitting cane : conversations with bamboo rodmakers / Ed Engle.
        p.   cm.
    ISBN 0-8117-0008-9
    1. Fishing rods—Design and construction. 2. Fly fishing. 3. Bamboo. I. Title.

SH452.E54 2002
688.7'9124—dc21   2002023066

    ISBN 978-0-8117-0008-5

CONTENTS

FOREWORD

IN HIS INTRODUCTION TO THIS BOOK, ED ENGLE SAYS IT WAS ME and our late friend Gil Lipp who first put a bamboo fly rod in his hand. I'm sure that's true and I'm happy to take partial credit for it, but the fact is that I don't actually remember the event, let alone what rod it could have been. (Memories that old sometimes get a little foggy.) What I do recall is that the three of us all got into bamboo fly rods at about the same time for roughly the same reasons.

Back then you had three choices in a fly rod: fiberglass, graphite, or bamboo. Fiberglass was the standard. It was common, serviceable, familiar, and affordable. It was what we grew up with, what most fishermen used, and most likely to be what you fished with if you didn't want to put a lot of money into your tackle or didn't really have an opinion about rod materials.

Graphite was new then, and it was still considered by many to be experimental. Fabulous claims were made for graphite rods (some of which turned out to be true), but these newfangled things looked too skinny, felt too stiff, and were black—like they'd been designed by the CIA. We wondered if they'd catch on.

Bamboo was old school, quietly high tone, and by then largely under the radar of the mass tackle market. Some say that the golden age of bamboo rods had ended, that they'd been largely overshadowed by glass and later graphite, and that the so-called bamboo rod renaissance was still a decade or two away, but the craftsmen who continued to make fine rods in those years—not to mention the fishermen who bought and fished them—would rightfully argue with that.

For most fishermen, bamboo wasn't the first choice in a fly rod then—any more than it is now—but to some of us it was irresistibly warm, natural, romantic, and reeking of craftsmanship and tradition. Magazine articles always pictured bamboo rods lying on rolltop desks next to an oil lamp and a worn leather fly wallet, all dimly lit through a gold filter. The best of them were great rods in their own right, but they also seemed to stand for something. We probably couldn't have said exactly what, but we knew we wanted in on it.

Ed, Gil, and I were in the middle of our misspent youths then and as crazed and idealistic as you could only be coming out of the 1960s, with most of your wits intact. We were honestly curious about bamboo, but we were also suckers for the romance. In other words, we were predisposed to like bamboo fly rods. The good ones turned out to cast beautifully, and that was that. There was no further discussion and no turning back.

Ed does lots of things in this book that I like, and one of them is that he pretty much leaves it at that. He doesn't try to sell you on bamboo or make claims for it over other materials (although if you can read some of his descriptions of how these rods cast and not begin to want one, you have a heart of stone).

In fact, Ed has the perfect temperament to write a book like this because he's a kind of practical romantic. He appreciates the craftsmanship and the nostalgia behind these rods—or the "hocus pocus" as he calls it—and he knows that no bamboo nut can ever be completely objective. He also thinks of them as instruments that are meant to be used—to the point that if you don't take them out and fish them, they're useless. He's not a collector except in the sense that he has more rods than he really needs, as most of us do after a lifetime of fishing.

I can testify that Ed fishes his bamboo rods and fishes them hard, not just on pretty little mountain streams, but also in gale force winds on prairie lakes in Nebraska. Hocus pocus notwithstanding, he fishes with bamboo rods because he likes the way they cast. All the other stuff is just gravy.

You see that when he writes about specific rods. His descriptions of how they look are meticulous and accurate, with attention to the kind of fine details many of us would miss, but it's when he starts casting them down at the park or fishing with them that he's likely to begin making allusions to sex.

In some ways this book is a personal essay, and in others it's pure journalism. Ed doesn't try to hide his enthusiasm (he probably couldn't even if he did try), but he also knows exactly when to sit back and let either the facts or the rodmakers say whatever it is they have to say. It helps that Ed is a good researcher, a keen observer, and the kind of unrepentant enthusiast who'll make a pilgrimage to a Tonkin bamboo plantation in China just to see where the stuff comes from. It also helps that he has a deep appreciation for eccentricity. In fact, some have even said that he's a little bit eccentric himself.

What you end up with is a close and often personal look at some rodmakers and some of their rods, as well as a penetrating peek into the subculture that produced them. As a group, bamboo rodmakers are people who have decided to do something for love instead of money, although, as Willie Nelson once said of musicians, they ain't above takin' the money. They also tend to cite the names of legendary old rodmakers as influences: Leonard, Payne, Garrison, Young, Dickerson. But beyond that, these people are one of a kind. Some try to be savvy about the business end of things and are making some kind of living from their rods. Others work real jobs and seem content to make rods on the side and at their own pace. Some sound like engineers when they talk about rods, and others sound like artists, or at least artistic engineers. Some are humble and others are, let's say, a little overconfident.

Of course, the differences show in their work. There are quick, powerful rods and soft, sensuous ones and the rare exceptional rod that will serenely and effortlessly do it all. Even the looks of the rod reflect the person who made it. One maker will labor long and hard to make a magnificent reel seat, while the next will say that a reel seat is just a glorified clamp and shouldn't be the focus of the rod.

The updates at the ends of the chapters are there partly in the interest of accuracy and partly to show how things can change in this kind of strange, solitary profession. One maker has all but abandoned a hard-won new process in favor of something more traditional; another is turning out more rods than ever; and still another has all but retired from rod making, but if you really want one of his rods, you can call him up and he'll talk about it.

The choice of rodmakers also seems to illustrate a point. A few of these people are already household names in bamboo rod circles and a few others will be soon, so it might be a good move to buy one of their rods now, before the price goes up.

This book could be the first place you'll hear about a rodmaker who will later go on to be famous—or at least as famous as you can get working in relative obscurity in a small backwater of the tackle business. But Ed is wise enough not to get into that. He knows that there are plenty of ways for even the best craftsmen to not "make it" (in the sense that we Americans use that term), and he also knows that in the long run the rods will speak for themselves.

—John Gierach

INTRODUCTION

MANY OF THE CHAPTERS IN *SPLITTING CANE* ORIGINALLY appeared in shortened versions in an obscure Montana fly-fishing magazine called *The Angler's Journal*. Bob Auger, the DePuy's Spring Creek river keeper at the time, started the magazine in 1994 with the idea of dedicating its contents to spring creek, still-water, and tailwater fly-fishing enthusiasts.

From the beginning, *The Angler's Journal* was different by design from the snazzier, higher-circulation fly-fishing magazines. It was truly a magazine published by fly fishers for fly fishers. Auger and Neil Travis, the editor, proclaimed it "the voice of quality angling," and it was. There were articles on aquatic entomology, fly patterns, fly tying, featured spring creeks, streamside ornithology, fly-fishing history, artist profiles, and the art of dry fly presentation. I liked the magazine because it wasn't a slick. Reading it was like running into a pal on the river and having a long conversation. In 1997, Auger sold his interest in the magazine to Mitch Hurt, Buck Crawford, and Rod Walinchus. At that time Rod took over the editorial duties.

A unique feature of the magazine was a regular column on bamboo fly rods that began with its first issue. Ardith Morgan originated the Cane Currents column, which presented an in-depth profile of a bamboo rodmaker in every issue. When Ardith was no longer able to continue the column, Bob Auger asked me if I'd like to take it on. I couldn't have asked for a better assignment. For the next five years, until the magazine ceased publication with the Winter 2000 issue, I test cast bamboo fly rods, interviewed the rodmakers, dabbled in buying vintage bamboo fly rods, and tested fly lines for bamboo rods. I dutifully reported my findings four times a year in the Cane Currents column.

I never really had a plan when I selected the rodmakers for the Cane Currents profiles. Sometimes I just got hold of a rod that I'd always wanted to cast, or maybe my friend and bamboo fly rod aficionado, John Gierach, would suggest a rodmaker's name, or perhaps a rod on the previously owned rack in Mike Clark's rod-building shop would catch my eye.

The sum of all the columns taken as a whole is a rather eclectic collection of rodmakers that gives a fair representation of bamboo rod making in America today. Most are full-time rodmakers. A few are part-time or semiretired. Some are experiencing a measure of success, while others are struggling. All are dedicated heart and soul to making fly rods out of bamboo.

The list of rodmaker names you see here is by no means all-inclusive. Those of you familiar with bamboo rods and rodmakers will see some familiar names and note the absence of others. You may also see some unfamiliar names. All of the included rods are inimitably fishable. As to one rod being better than another, I leave that to the fly fishers. The uniqueness of bamboo as a rod- making material is that it lends itself to so many interpretations of how a rod should cast, play a fish, and feel in the hand. You must cast the rod to know.

I followed a simple protocol when I researched these rodmaker profiles. I either borrowed a rod from a friend (John Gierach had a stack of them) or asked the rodmaker to lend me a rod that he thought best represented his work. When I received the rod, I'd test cast it on the lawn. In a few cases I actually fished the rod. After I cast the rod, I called the rodmaker and interviewed him at length. My idea was to elicit in the rodmaker's own words what it is that inspires him to make fly rods from bamboo and how he goes about translating that inspiration into a finished fly-fishing tool.

I got much more than I expected from the interviews. Over the years I've kept in touch with many of the rodmakers I interviewed. Mostly we talk on the telephone every couple of months, but in a few cases we've managed to go fishing together. I value all the friendships, and in the process, I think I've learned a little of the secret life of rodmakers.

One rodmaker announced that he'd come up with an undiscovered new taper. He said that if I didn't believe him I should call another rodmaker we both knew and ask him about it. I did indeed make the call, and it turns out that the other rodmaker had measured ("miked") the taper. He verified that it was "something I've never seen and I've miked a lot of rods" and went on to say that the rod cast nicely, too. I called the rodmaker back, apologized, and asked how he'd come up with the taper.

"This isn't for public knowledge, but I was drunk at the time," he said.

After I told my friend John Gierach the story, he wryly commented that he'd heard a lot of tales about new tapers being discovered and that invariably they proved to be untrue, but that under the circumstances "this is the only one I believe."

Another rodmaker told me that people have asked him to pass judgment on other rodmakers' work, but that he refused to do it. He said he'd comment if there was something good about the rod, but that "you have to take a lot of stuff into consideration, like whether it's a Friday or whether the guy needs a paycheck or whether the guy's just starting out." He said that if a person is serious about rod making and sticks with it, he will just get better and better and better. I agree with him.

Still another rodmaker commented that it's the return customers that keep him in business. "They often become pretty good friends and you fish with them and they share things with you that they wouldn't share with another vendor, so to speak. We're doing something for them that makes them feel good," he said.

Bamboo fly rods make me feel good, too. I like the idea that there are men and women all across the United States and the world sizing up culms of Tonkin cane in their home workshops and then handcrafting these gorgeous fishing tools out of it. I like that they put their names on the rods when they're finished and tell you that if you ever have a problem with the rod to bring it back to them and they'll take care of it. And I like the idea that once in a while it's difficult to get in touch with a rodmaker because he's out on the river. You can't do enough taper design research.

This book would not have been possible without the support of Bob Auger, Rod Walinchus, Buck Crawford, Mitch Hurt, and *The Angler's Journal*. I am also indebted to Jim Butler, Paul Guernsey, and *Fly Rod & Reel* magazine for publishing in somewhat different form several of the stories that appear here. In addition, I would like to recognize Terry Yamagishi for his translations of several of the chapters that appeared in *Fly Fisherman Magazine—JAPAN EDITION*.

There would be nothing on the page at all if John Gierach and the late Gil Lipp hadn't stuck a bamboo fly rod in my hand thirty years ago and said, "Cast this!" John continues to this day to call me and say, "You gotta cast this one. When can you get up here?" The other required ingredient in the making of this book has been the friendship of A. K. Best, who is a true fly-fishing master.

Three other people have made important contributions to this work. Jana Rush is my sweetheart, wife, fly-fishing companion, on-river watercolorist, and fellow explorer of China's Tonkin cane forests. Bernice Engle, along with being my mother, former librarian, and tireless cheerleader for those who write books, is responsible for much that is good in my life. My sister, Carolyn Reyes, possesses among her numerous gifts more natural fishing talent than anyone I know.

And finally, my thanks to all the rodmakers. You light up my days on the water.

—Ed Engle

CHAPTER ONE

W. E. Carpenter Rod Company

August 1998. There is a storm brewing up the canyon from the town park where I am standing with a gorgeous W. E. Carpenter Browntone 7-foot, 4-weight bamboo fly rod. The rod has that deep, even walnut hue that is characteristic of the browntoning process. The nodes, which come out a lighter, golden color when the rod is browntoned, further accentuate the richness of the cane.

I'm pretty happy that I got to cast a Carpenter rod at all. When I telephoned Walt Carpenter to see if I could get hold of one of his rods to cast, he said that he had "some Paynes and a Leonard" scattered around the house but no Carpenters. He said he'd do what he could to "scare one up" and give me a call. As it turned out, he was able to borrow a Carpenter from the collection of his friend Mike Robinson. That's the rod I'm holding in my hand.

Walt Carpenter

PHOTO BY CHIKAKO MORI DESIGNS

I begin running the rod through my standard series of tests. The rod certainly doesn't have any problems casting close in. The leader forms a nice, fully controllable loop with just 5 feet of the double taper 4-weight line out from the tip-top guide. At 10 feet of fly line out, it's casting smooth as silk.

The real ecstasy begins after I've worked out about 30 feet of line. That's when I realize that no shock waves are forming in the loops. None at all. I crank out another 10 feet of line, and the loops hold perfect and smooth and wonderful. I think to myself that it's this smoothness, this silkiness that I always seem to be searching for in a rod. If you are one of those casters, like I am, who believes that a fly rod can actually be sexy, this is as sensuous as it gets.

I have felt this way before. It's happened with several Payne rods and with a wonderful 7½-foot, 5-weight J. A. Bradford rod that John Gierach let me cast on the Frying Pan River several years ago. The Carpenter and the Bradford both seemed to capture whatever it was that Jim Payne was able to put into his rods.

There is a unique feel to casting the Carpenter. It's a kind of nudge that you sense in the butt section and even into the upper part of the grip. When you feel that, it seems like the rest of the rod follows it perfectly, and that in turn is transferred down through the rest of the taper. And it is the taper that oils those loops so smoothly. I could go on all day about it, but let's just say it's a feeling you don't forget.

You must understand that this is not a rod to trifle with when it comes to casting. You must learn that it's not some graphite stick that you can overpower the hell out of without consequence. If you beat up on the rod, everything falls apart. You must cast it. If you discipline yourself to work together with the rod, it takes care of you.

The next surprise comes when the storm moves in closer and occasional breezy gusts come up. I cast the line directly into the wind, and the loop holds nicely while laying the leader straight out. I then turn ninety degrees and cast the rod in the crosswind. The line still lays out straight with very little drift.

Before I am done, I find that casts to 50 feet are effortless and can be placed with accuracy and delicacy. Casts to 70 feet maintain their grace. I figure I could perhaps go farther, but don't see the need. A rod of this type, at least for me, has no reason to be out farther than 70 feet.

Besides, the rain is now coming down in sheets. I pack the rod up, head home, and give Walt Carpenter a call.

"I'm glad you noticed that," Walt said, referring to what I described as the little nudge in the butt section of the rod.

"I call that the afterburner, and it's a bit of a secret. I take great pride in the action of the rod. Sure, the cosmetics are very nice, and I think the rods are well balanced, but it comes down to how it casts. And I can't really take credit for that. My current tapers are more Thomas, Payne, Edwards, Hawes, Carpenter tapers. You change them a bit here and there . . . but it all comes out of the Hudson Valley or Catskill school of rod making, and that all goes back to Leonard. You're talking to a guy who does it the same way as Hiram Leonard and Jim Payne did," he said.

Carpenter said that awhile back a customer of his called and said that his rods "almost cast themselves."

"He hit on the essence of what I try to put into a fly rod. They do have that little kick, that afterburner, and if you don't push them they will almost cast themselves, but it's not like a parabolic config-uration. It's a very complicated set of tapers. If you miked the rod, you'd see a whole series of compounds. They are very difficult tapers to cut into bamboo, but they are very progressive. You always have that power to call on if you are capable of making it happen. Even the 7-footer has quite a bit of power," he said.

Carpenter said that he has been most influenced by Jim Payne because of the integrity of the Payne rod.

"Jim Payne was the very best rodmaker because he could do everything. I don't know of any other rodmaker—and I've been a serious student of rod making for thirty years—who has done it better. Everything Payne did was understated, which was like the man himself, and it was done for a reason. Everything on a Payne rod could be defended . . . the color, the finish, the preservatives, the way he treated his wood, the ferrules. And the physical impression the rod gave you showed it," he said.

Carpenter also said that he liked Leonards, but that the Paynes embodied the very best of cane rods.

"In general, the Leonards were a little more forgiving because the action was somewhat slower, which might have made fishing them a bit easier. But again, and I'm talking in generalities, the Payne was more toward a medium-fast action, which made it more of a casting rod, but if you could cast the fly with it, you were going to be able to catch fish," he said.

Carpenter said that he has fooled around with rods for most of his life, but he began to take it seriously when the well-known Catskill flytiers, Harry and Elsie Darbee, encouraged him to build rods.

"One thing came to another, and I built a rod and it turned out pretty good. That's when I started to wonder if I could make another," he said.

Carpenter said there were no popularly available books on rod building when he started out, but Elsie Darbee turned up a few for him to look at.

"The Darbee's shop was a wonderful place then. It was open to all. There were anglers, writers, you name it. We all gathered there. And Harry had a box of used rods. There were Garrisons, Gillums, Leonards, and Paynes, and he allowed me to take them home and cast them. I paid him back by doing rod restoration work for the privilege. Eventually, the relationship turned into a whole lot more for me. The Darbees were like parents," he said.

Carpenter went on to work for the Leonard and Payne rod companies and continued to build rods on the side. He eventually opened his own shop in 1980.

Along the way he acquired a bevelling machine from rodmaker Sam Carlson that another respected rodmaker, F. E. Thomas, had built in 1890. It had initially been used to make the Kosmic rods.

"The beveller is wonderful. It's very precise. It allows you to reproduce tapers with a high degree of accuracy and consistency. You have to remember that when the beveller was built people were building rods for a living. They didn't want to produce just one rod off a set of V blocks; they wanted to make dozens. Just the idea of automating the process is amazing to me. The Maine State Museum has been trying to get me to donate the beveller to them, but I can't because it's how I make my living," Carpenter said.

Carpenter related how the beveller came with a set of thirty steel taper patterns that were hand filed to make rods ranging from double-built deep-sea tuna rods to very lightweight and varied fly rods.

"The steel taper patterns were empirically developed. The guys would file a little bit and then make six strips and go out on the casting platform and try them. If the rod didn't work, they'd go back and file a little more. There are thousands of man-hours in them. I've altered some by wedging them, but I've never destroyed an original. They could not be resurrected," Carpenter said.

Carpenter currently makes about twenty-five rods a year. Available rods include the Special, Browntone, Browntone Classic, Mahogany, a series of Exhibition Grade rods, and the newest addition, called the Highlands Special. Most of the rods are available in two and three pieces in a variety of lengths. Most models can be built in light dry fly, medium dry fly, or medium-fast action.

"When you get right down to it, rod actions are basically slow, medium, and fast. My light dry fly action has a delicate taper and is fine tipped. It's best suited to light line weights and smaller flies. The medium dry fly is a little faster and is best described as an evenly arcing rod. If you hooked a good fish on it and stood back and looked at the rod, it would bend in an almost even arc. The medium fast has a stiffer butt with more of a progressive action. It's more of a true parabola, which means it bends more in the upper third and that speeds it up," he said.

The Browntone is currently the most popular Carpenter rod, but the Mahogany follows it closely.

The 7-foot, 4-weight Browntone I cast has three-around node staggering, which is standard on Carpenter rods. Carpenter uses pre-embargo butt-cut Tonkin cane on all his rods. The reel seat on the rod I cast was a sliding band with a mortised walnut spacer. There is a knurled cork check to delineate the cork grip, which is best described as a slightly tapered cigar. The wraps above the winding check are chestnut tipped in black, gold, and then red. Line guides are wrapped in chestnut tipped in black. All wraps on Carpenter's rods are done by his wife, Marcia. The stripping guide is traditional tungsten carbide.

Carpenter keeps alive the Hudson Valley rod-building tradition by producing his own 18 percent nickel silver step-down ferrules in his shop. He also makes all the reel seat hardware. The hardware on the rod I cast is oxidized to a deep black. The tip section ferrules in the two-piece rod are wrapped in chestnut and tipped black, gold, and red. Tip sections are delineated by one or two dots and the serial number of the rod. The serial number also appears on the butt section near the ferrule.

The first two digits of the five-digit serial number indicate the year the rod was built. The third digit specifies the order in which the rod was built in a given year. The first rod of the year is designated with the numeral 1. The final two digits indicate the length of the rod. The rod is signed "W. E. Carpenter, Maker" on the butt.

"I try to keep the writing as much away from the eye as possible so you can see the bamboo. I think my penmanship is good and it doesn't intrude, but I keep it to a minimum. If I wrote a story on there, it would intrude," Carpenter said.

The rods are noted for a superlative varnish finish.

"I use Valspar #10 Spar Varnish, which is getting harder to obtain," he said. He then added that how he applies the varnish is one of the little secrets he keeps to himself. Options are available on standard models, and special orders are accepted.

"I do offer options, but I'm getting more and more into what might be called commissioned rods," he said.

Carpenter is making fewer rods now than in the past. "I have a pretty good tackle business, so I don't make as many rods. It's kind of a limited production," he said.

In the meantime, he is fishing more. "I'm a good caster, probably a whole lot better caster than fisherman, but I've got a buddy trying to make me a fisherman this year, so I'm going nuts over fishing."

Nonetheless, I think it's safe to assume that you will continue to see Carpenter rods. They represent the finest rods being made today in the Hudson Valley rod-building tradition.

"I make traditional bamboo rods. The art peaked in the 1930s. It was the state of the art then, and it is the state of the art now. It's hard to want to change that," he said.

Carpenter said that when everything is considered, it always comes back to the bamboo.

"We take this natural pole of grass, tear it apart, and then put it back together in a form we want, but it's still very natural. The only unnatural part is we've added a taper that's different from nature and some glue. That's it. We're really trying to complement nature. And a bamboo rod is a wonderful way to do that."

That, I think, is as close as you'll come to explaining the essence and the art of building a cane rod.

May 2001. "I'm getting close to retiring. I hope that in the next year and a half to two years I'll be able to stop taking orders," Walt Carpenter said. "I'm not going to stop building rods, but I'm going to be quite selective about the orders I take. I'm hoping that will let me slow down a bit."

Carpenter figures that if you count the rods he made at Payne, Leonard, and Carpenter that he'll have made about a thousand rods "by the time I get done."

"That's about four hundred thousand hours of work. The life of a professional rodmaker doesn't leave you too much time for fun," he chuckled.

Carpenter said that one of the reasons he's considering not taking too many more orders is that he already has a lot now and that it can get a bit overwhelming. Many of the standing orders are from fly fishers who have bought Carpenter rods in the past.

"I have one customer who orders four rods at a time. That's great security for me," he said.

Carpenter said that he's simplified the rod models he is now offering. Orders are no longer being taken for the Highlands Special, but the Browntone and Mahogany models are still available.

"I've changed what I offer every once in awhile over the years. I think you have to be willing to change in order to stay in business. I just try to make the rods better and better," he said.

For my part, and I know it's a bit selfish, I hope Walt Carpenter never stops making fly rods.

CHAPTER TWO

J. A. Bradford Company

May 1997. Every September I meet my pals—John Gierach, A. K. Best, Mike Clark, and other assorted incorrigibles—for the blue-winged olive hatch on Colorado's Frying Pan River. Like all anglers on all fishing trips, I go for the trout, the hatch, the company, and the river. But in this case there is another reason why I go. It seems like every year John Gierach brings a cane rod that I fall in love with.

Last year John introduced me to an elegant honey-colored 7½-foot, 3½-ounce J. A. Bradford rod. We were standing by a favorite pool waiting for rises when John said, "Here, try this," and handed me the fly rod. He had that serious little smile on his face that he gets when he knows something like the fishing or a rod or the way the sun is shining is just right.

I took the fly rod. I could tell it was a sweetheart within two or three false casts. It cast effortlessly, but even more amazing was

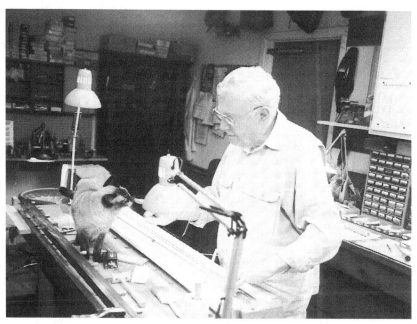

John Bradford

the fact that I wasn't throwing any shock waves at all as I false cast the line out. That's unusual for me. I have a tendency to over-power fly rods, especially when working line out. It typically results in a shock wave or two until I get enough line out to load the rod. It didn't happen with the Bradford rod. Casting it was literally as smooth as silk—with a little oil added for good measure.

It's the kind of casting experience you can only get from a classic moderate dry fly action. And if you have ever cast a Jim Payne fly rod, you will feel him lurking about in the Bradford rod. There is a distinctive but indescribable feel when casting a Payne. It takes place between the handle and the stripping guide, and you know it if you've experienced it. The spirit of that experience is in the Bradford. The fly rod simply came alive in my hand.

I should also say that while I was fiddling around casting it, a fine rainbow trout came up and ate the dry fly. I was hooked.

More recently, I imposed on John to allow me to take the rod out and cast it on the grass without the distraction of trout jumping out of the Frying Pan River to take a fly cast by it.

The rod, which is called the Legacy, still allowed me to cast a loop without shock waves. It became even more clear that this smoothness comes from the sensible dry fly action. That action also makes casting close in with just the leader or a few feet of fly line out a breeze. Within actual fishing ranges from 10 to 40 feet, the rod is exceedingly accurate. Actually, it's the most accurate 5-weight fly rod I've cast in many years. Once again, ascribe this to the action.

In addition, the rod casts effortlessly to around 50 feet and with a bit of a haul will reach out to 65 feet. I suspect it will cast even farther, but there is really no reason for it. The Legacy has trout rod written all over it, and the best trout-casting ranges where I live are less than 40 feet. Accuracy is the name of the game with our trout, and the Legacy is a real player in that department.

Many cane rod aficionados know John Bradford as a master restorer of classic cane rods rather than as a rod builder.

"Actually, I started off building cane rods. I lived right on the Pere Marquette River in Michigan. I was guiding fishermen when I was twelve and built my first rod with my uncle's help when I was fourteen," said Bradford.

He said that he met master rod builders Paul Young, who lived nearby, and Lyle Dickerson when he was growing up.

"I knew these guys and could go over to their houses once in awhile. They really weren't very tolerant of a thirteen-year-old kid, but they let me in," Bradford said.

Bradford later joined the Air Force and after a thirty-year military career started a rod-building business with a partner.

"We got a contract with Abercrombie and Fitch to build a lot of graphite rods. We built a few cane rods, too. During that time is when I began to get the reputation for restoring bamboo rods, which I was doing on the side," he said.

More recently Bradford has gotten out of the graphite rod-building business because it "got too crazy" and limited the number of rods he would restore to just a few a year.

"I get a lot of calls to restore rods, but I don't do much of it anymore. I don't know how I pick the ones I do. It's sort of an arbitrary decision. The other day this eighty-year-old guy called. He fishes every day and said my rod restorations were the best he'd ever seen. He wanted me to do his rod. I agreed. I charged him only $170. It's kinda fun when you get someone like that," Bradford said.

Bradford's passion now is building his own rods. I asked him about the Legacy. "You're not alone in not throwing shock waves with that rod. You may think you cast differently, but I've had a lot of people comment on the feel of that rod," he said.

Bradford said that Legacy is actually just a name rather than an official rod model. He builds the Legacy in lengths from 6 feet 9 inches to 8 feet for 3-weight to 6-weight lines. Most of the rods are two-piece, although he does build some three-piece rods.

"Really, what's in a name? Names are names. It's kind of like the Grangers and the Heddons. They had so many different names, but what's really the difference between a Black Beauty and a Bill Stanley's Favorite? I build another rod I call the Talisman, but the only real difference between it and the Legacy is that it doesn't have an agate stripping guide. I'm thinking about naming one the Specialist, too," he said.

Bradford said the best place to start when talking about the details of his rods is with the two hardest things to get when building a cane rod.

"The bamboo I use is old stuff, maybe forty or fifty years old. You can't get it anymore. I got some of it from Walt Powell, and some of it is so old that it's pre-embargo. I probably got enough to last my lifetime, but when it's gone, it's probably gone forever. There's no hope of getting this kind of bamboo anymore because the people growing it want to get rid of it real quick and make money. All the rodmakers are complaining about green bamboo," he said.

Bradford said that the other hard-to-get item for rod builders is good cork. He carefully selects the cork rings for his rod handles and often culls 50 percent of what he sees.

"It now costs me $30 to make a cork grip because I cull so much. At seventy cents a cork ring, it adds up. I could end up culling as much as 80 percent soon, and that could get almost cost prohibitive," he said.

In an overall view, the Legacy possesses a striking but simple elegance. Its sparse, functional details add to the rod's beauty.

The rod I cast was fitted with a nickel silver-pocketed cap with sliding band reel seat. A nickel silver cork check was also included. The hardware is made by Research Engineering Corporation (REC) to Bradford's specifications and stamped with his logo. The wood spacer is Bird's-Eye Maple that Bradford meticulously stains with water-soluble aniline dye.

"The water-soluble aniline dye is the most difficult to work with, but I am able to get the most striking contrast possible when I use it," he said.

The wood spacer is round in reel seats where the pocketed cap hardware is used. Bradford also makes an E. F. Payne–type reel seat where the spacer is flattened on the bottom. The butt cap on this reel seat is straight rather than pocketed. The reel foot fits up into the cap where the spacer has been flattened.

"I use almost exclusively sliding band–type reel seats, but I can do an uplock or downlock. I don't really think they are necessary for the size rods I'm specializing in, though," he said.

Bradford bronzes all reel seat hardware, the unique six-sided or hexed winding check, the stripping guide, the line guides, the ferrules, and the tip-top guide.

"You'll see it in the right light. It looks like a penny. I bronze the hardware so that it blends with the wraps and the wood," he said.

The agate stripping guides were obtained from John Weir in the 1970s. The line guides are tungsten, and the tip-top guide is a Perfection with a nickel silver tube and tungsten ring.

The exquisite cigar cork grip is $6^{1}/_{8}$ inches long with a $^{31}/_{32}$-inch diameter at its widest point, which is one-third of the way up from the butt.

"For some reason the $^{31}/_{32}$-inch grip diameter just feels good. Everyone likes it. I go to a lot of trouble to get it. Even $^{1}/_{16}$ inch over makes the rod feel different. There really is something about it," Bradford commented.

The ring-style hook keeper is one of several hundred that Bradford obtained from either the Payne or Leonard company in the mid-1960s.

Bradford uses nickel silver Super SD (step-down) style ferrules (also called truncated or spigot ferrules) built by Classic Sporting Enterprises, Inc. (CSE). The ferrules and the butt cap are pinned.

"I think these ferrules look more traditional. I don't hold with the theory that truncated ferrules weaken the wood. There are an awful lot of Paynes, Leonards, and Orvis rods out there that all have pinned truncated ferrules," he said.

Bradford wraps the guides in desert gold silk tipped with pale yellow silk.

"I picked those colors because they are very similar to a brownish color E. C. Powell used years and years ago that he called desert gold," he said.

Bradford's sparse signature wraps are similar to those used by Lyle Dickerson.

"Dickerson used to make the first wrap 8 inches above the winding check and a second one at 10 inches. On what he called his guide's model fly rod, there was a third wrap at 12 inches. I guess he figured the guides caught bigger fish. Anyway, I thought it looked a little plain down there on my rods, but I didn't want it to get too fancy, so I picked up on these wraps. I put them at 8, 10, and 12 inches on all the Legacies," Bradford said.

The two tips for the Legacy are differentiated by an extra off-set pale yellow wrap on both ends of one tip.

Bradford uses a straight beveller to initially get the bamboo strips to sixty degrees and then hand planes them to the final stage. He prefers opposing node staggering on his rods. In this arrangement a node on one strip is adjacent to two clear strips followed by another node, which is adjacent to two clear strips.

"Rodmakers can argue all day over how to stagger the nodes. I like opposing nodes because I think it's a good compromise, but I have used other node staggering systems. The opposing node gives you a node on opposite sides of the rod. I feel that gives you a strength factor that is just a little better. It isn't an uncommon arrangement. E. C. Powell used it and Walt Powell still uses it. It also saves bamboo and that's important nowadays," Bradford said.

The heart of Bradford's Legacy rod is a taper that creates a fluid medium-action rod.

"I don't like drastic tapers. Some new-generation bamboo rod builders are tending to try to replicate graphite and that's a mistake. If you want graphite, get graphite. What I'm looking for is a medium-action rod that doesn't throw waves and will deliver a fly with great delicacy at modest distances. We don't need to cast to the far side of the Columbia River," he said.

Bradford said that he doesn't experiment much with tapers.

"I'm sixty-eight years old, and I don't have time to be starting out with new experimental tapers. My tapers and rod lengths are the result of all the experience I've had with Dickerson rods, which were quite strong, and Paul Young rods, which I never really cared for that much, and all the other rods I've come across over the years," he said.

Bradford said that fifteen years ago he thought Leonards were the measure of all cane rods.

"It seemed like everything else was a little better or not as good as a Leonard. So they served as a useful measure. But in recent years my mind has changed. The Leonards seem too wimpy now. Maybe it's because they're so old or maybe the tapers aren't right. Anyway, now I measure everything by what a Payne is," he said.

Bradford said his tapers are initially predicated on Payne tapers for two-piece or three-piece rods.

"Those tapers and the rod lengths I use keep me in a limited area. I don't worry about other rods. I stick to my little area of expertise. Over the years I've tried in my humble way to get that special feel that a Payne has," Bradford said.

And he's done that and more. He puts a fly fisher's life into every rod he builds.

"I had a pretty good background in fly fishing and didn't know there was any other way of life" is the way John Bradford puts it.

April 2001. John Bradford said that at seventy-two years of age he's still taking orders on rods.

"I don't offer the Talisman anymore. Almost all of what I'm making now are the Legacies. I'm still tweaking things a little here and there, but I really haven't changed much in the rods. If I do find a better way to do something, I do it. When something different does come up, I always ask myself will it do a job better and/or faster? If it will make you do it better, it's worth doing it. If it will make you do it faster but not better, it's worth considering. If it does both, grab it," he said.

John Bradford is always looking for ways to improve his rods. Recently he noted improvements in Bailey Woods hardware, so he's switched over to using it. Conversely, he hasn't switched from what have become his trademark step-down ferrules to what seems like the universally popular Super-Z-type ferrule.

"Quite frankly, step-down ferrules are harder to get on the blank. I think Garrison recommended the Super-Z-type ferrule—it really is a fine ferrule, and everyone just started using it. Garrison's rationale was that you don't have to take off the extra wood under the ferrule if you use a Super-Z and therefore it will be stronger, but that's not true. I've never seen a rod broken at the ferrule; they break below it or above it. The fact is that with the Super-Z ferrule you don't have to go through that tedious process of doing a step-down on the bamboo inside the ferrule. The only reason I do it is for cosmetic reasons. I just think the step-down ferrule looks better. That's why I keep it," Bradford said.

The trick is to pay attention to every rod that you make, and that is what John Bradford does.

"The school of rod making is evolving, and the guy who is evolving it is the person who is never satisfied. I like to think that I am one of those persons," Bradford said.

CHAPTER THREE

The Hidy Rod Company

IT'S LATE SEPTEMBER IN THE ROCKY MOUNTAINS, AND I'M fishing a little stream called Goose Creek. I can tell you the name because there are enough Goose Creeks in the Rockies to keep you off my trail. I've fished this particular Goose Creek for close to twenty-five years.

Right now the sharply honed light is cutting open the landscape. September light can make places you've known for twenty-five years appear bright, crisp, and new.

I'm fishing a Jim Hidy 7½-foot, 3-weight rod. It was made for streams like Goose Creek, which is never more than 20 feet across at this time of year. The water's running clear and thin. Presentations have to be close in and accurate. The idea is to cast a #18 Royal Wulff into the run outs below the pools and along the foamy fringes around the pockets. To neutralize drag, cast close, keep the rod tip up, and guide the fly through the riffles.

Jim Hidy

The Hidy rod does this and more with grace. The rod traces its roots to E. C. Powell, who pioneered a unique school of semi-hollow bamboo rod construction that has remained centered on the West Coast for the past sixty years. Jim Hidy's rod follows Powell's semihollow tradition.

The weight-reducing importance of semihollow design is obvious when in larger rods, but its lure is a bit more subtle in a 7½-foot, 3-weight rod. You notice it first on the false cast. The line moves fluidly with few shock waves.

Even more subtle is the response of the whole rod to the casting stroke. The somewhat lighter overall weight of the rod coupled with its taper means that the rod tends to dampen more quickly, resulting in a cast that just feels brighter and crisper.

Needless to say, this effect increases with rods designed for 4-, 5-, and 6-weight lines.

Several days before I fished the rod, I'd field tested it on the grass at a local park. It was a dream to cast in close. The very fine tip allows the rod to load up a bit quicker, which means you feel it with little or no fly line out beyond the tip-top guide. It's what you need on streams like Goose Creek.

The rod casts effortlessly at real trout-fishing ranges out to 30 or 35 feet. Beyond that it's easy to cast the line to 50 feet as long as you keep in mind that it is a 3-weight rod and it can be overpowered if you bludgeon it. Actually, I didn't have much trouble casting close to 60 feet with a snappy single haul, but that was as far as I tried. There is really no reason to cast this rod beyond 40 feet, but I suspect a full-line-in-the-air fly-casting crazy might be able to get it out to 75 or even 80 feet. But that would be a crime. The beauty of this rod is that it makes casting close-in fun. You feel it load. The rod forms graceful loops when the leader alone is cast.

What more can you ask for in a 3-weight?

"I believe in fine tips, hollowing, and rods that aren't too fast. The real trick is to make a rod that's fun to fish right in close to you," Jim Hidy said.

Hidy tried out the hollowing techniques pioneered by E. C. Powell on the third rod he built.

"Once I got on to the hollow rods, there was no turning back for me because the benefits so outweigh those of solid rods," Hidy said.

The semihollow rods, also known as chambered rods, are created by scrapping out the inner pith of the bamboo strip while retaining the outer power fibers. This reduces the overall rod weight.

Although the size of the chambers may vary in any given rod, all chambered rods utilize internal bridges or dams between the chambers. At the dams the pith is left intact at a precise location on each strip. When the strips are glued together, it's imperative that the dams meet up perfectly to form a solid wall between the chambers.

"I've developed a hollowing machine that I can adjust to take out as much depth as I want and still retain the necessary amount of power fibers from the bamboo. I can also adjust the length I want the dams to be. I like to get them down to $1/8$ to $3/16$ inch. It's important for them to be as small as possible and to meet up perfectly when you glue the strips. This will provide the necessary internal strength and prevent dead spots in the action," Hidy said.

Builders agree that the most difficult aspect of making the semihollow rod occurs when the strips are glued together. If too much glue is used, it will fill the chambers. Not enough glue could result in lifts or a loss in structural integrity.

"It's tricky. You have to brush on just the right amount of glue. When you are starting out in rod building, the only way to really tell how you're doing on the glue job is to build a rod and then cut it open to see what it looks like inside. And I can tell you that the last thing an apprentice rod builder wants to do is cut open a rod he just built," Hidy said.

Hidy said that he leaves the rod solid at the ferrule and "for some distance beyond that, depending on the particular rod," to provide integrity and strength.

"I hollow my three-piece rods out right up to the second ferrule. I keep the tips solid even though I might be able to take a little weight out because you need the weight to bend the rod, unless it's a large rod, which I don't build," Hidy said.

Hidy's rods are available for 2-weight through 6-weight lines in both solid and hollow designs.

"I don't make 8-weights because I don't fish 8-weights. I won't build any rod you want because I don't think you can just copy a taper and throw it on a rod you're not familiar with. You need to develop an empirical feel for the tapers. You can't just build rods that you haven't tested. That's why I stick to the line weights and tapers I know," he said.

Hidy said that the cutoff point for hollowed rods is at a 3-weight line.

"I can make a 3-weight rod either solid or hollow. When you get down to the 2-weights, there just isn't enough material in there to hollow out," he said.

Hidy doesn't make what could be called a standard model rod, but rather works within certain guidelines, unless a customer makes a special request. The three-piece 7½-foot rod I cast is representative of his work.

He used blond cane, which he prefers, but he has made darker rods in the past. The blued nickel silver reel seat utilizes a sliding band with a straight butt cap. Hidy machines the hardware himself. The fit of the sliding ring to the maple spacer is among the best I've seen. There is absolutely no slop. The spacer is flattened to accept the reel foot.

"I have a good supply of maple, but I sometimes use walnut for the spacers. If somebody brings me a piece of wood for the spacer, I will look at it and use it if possible. I like sticking to the hardwoods," Hidy said.

Hidy's preference for a smaller grip spooked me at first because I have large, long hands, but I was surprised at how comfortable the twelve-ring 5½-inch-long cork grip was when I cast the rod. I credit this to its half wells design. The pitch up to the flare under the thumb is very subtle and worked wonderfully for me compared to the short cigar grips most often encountered on very light rods.

In addition to reel seat hardware, Hidy also makes the ring-style hook keeper, which is strategically located above the handle.

The Hidy rods typically utilize the Perfection-style stripping guide. The color of the guide wraps vary. The rod I cast was brown tipped with black. The signature wraps are three very thin narrowly detached black wraps located approximately 2½ inches above the cork grip. The two tips are differentiated by black tipping on one of the tip-top wraps.

"I don't have any standard color threads that I wrap the guides with, but I won't use color combinations that I don't like. Typically, I use red, green, brown, or clear," Hidy said.

The wraps are sealed with epoxy, as is the flared end of the half wells cork grip.

The rod is signed "Hidy" on one strip. A serial number that corresponds to the rod's taper is designated on another strip. An "H" in the serial number denotes that the rod is of semihollow design.

Hidy uses Super-Z ferrules that are blued or bright in deference to the customer's wishes. Node staggering on the rod is three and three on the butt section and midsection, but changes to a spiral stagger on the tips for added strength. The rod projects an overall sense of quiet elegance. The accouterments are subdued, which allows the eye to be drawn to the beauty of the cane itself. Hidy's ultimate concern is how his rods perform.

"I was particularly lucky to learn the art of rod building from Jim Schaaf and Mario Wojnicki. They both build hollow rods, but they also have this overall sense of what a cane rod should do. The bottom line is that a fly rod must be able to cast the line, set the hook, and play a fish," Hidy said.

Hidy is among a minority of full-time bamboo rod builders who hand plane the entire rod.

"I just feel you get a higher quality rod when you hand plane. Even though some bevellers are close to medical quality standards today, you still lose control when you push the cane into the machine. You don't get the high degree of diligence that's required when you hand plane. Hand planing requires attention all the time," he said.

The importance of hand planing to Hidy is that the work can be checked throughout the process.

"You can get exact triangles and accurate tapers with today's machines, but I still like the idea of being able to hold a strip up to the light every couple of passes and checking to see where the fibers are going. I know that the fiber that is right under the reel seat is going to be the one that's in the center of the tip-top when I'm done because I can keep checking it throughout the entire process. A machine may cut a 100 percent accurate triangle, but it can't track a single fiber," Hidy said.

All of this dedication to the art of building cane rods comes through a long family association with fly fishing. Hidy's cousin was Vernon S. "Pete" Hidy who wrote the classic *The Art of Tying the Wet Fly and Fishing the Flymph*, which detailed Jim Leisenring's ideas, attitudes, and techniques of tying and fishing wet flies. Jim Hidy himself lived right across the street from the Golden Gate Angler's Casting Club for fourteen years.

"I got to see a lot of good arms and listen to current debate on fly rod design. A lot of the people who were involved with designing rods for the big rod companies would show up. What I liked most of all was that I could take a rod down there and put it in the hands of a great caster and see what it did," Hidy said.

It all contributed to Hidy's ultimate respect for how a rod feels when you cast it.

"Cosmetics are necessary and important, but a reel seat does not make a rod. It's the sum total of everything you put into it. I know that it's hard to hand plane good rods if you aren't in a good frame of mind. The whole expression of what you're putting out depends on your inspiration and how good you feel about it. I could probably crank a rod out in fifteen or twenty hours, but it takes a hundred hours because of everything else that goes into it," Hidy said.

And that might just be the reason why fishing Jim Hidy's bamboo fly rod on an autumn day on Goose Creek when the light is bright and crisp and everything looks brand new seems like the perfect thing to be doing.

Two years after Goose Creek and the delicate afternoon I spent with Jim Hidy's 7½-foot, 3-weight rod, a Hidy 8-footer for a 6-weight line arrived on the doorstep. The rod is the product of an ongoing telephone friendship that Jim and I have developed. We call each other to talk about tapers, casting, fly-fishing, and bamboo. The idea that I should have a 6-weight semihollow fly rod was born during those conversations. It's a fly rod that will hopefully fish the gamut of Rocky Mountain water with possible light warm-water applications. The rod arrived with a single tip and a simple explanation.

"The baby got the other tip. What I can I say?" Jim commented over the telephone with a hint of a new father's pride in his voice. "I'll get you a spare when I can."

The rod is another glorious example of Jim's work that in many ways is just a big-brother version of the 7½-foot rod. The nickel silver reel seat hardware is blued. The thrifty sliding band and straight butt cap with flattened maple spacer echo the lighter 3-weight, as does the thin, slightly longer thirteen-ring 6-inch half wells cork grip, which is basically a concession to my big hand. The rest is the same as the 3-weight—the handmade ring-style hook keeper, signature wraps, Perfection stripping guide, brown wraps tipped with black at the female ferrules, blued Super-Z ferrules, and the unique three-and-three node spacing on the butt and midsections, with the spiral stagger on the tip. The thrift incorporated in the thin grip, basic reel seat hardware, and clean elegant line of the rod gives the illusion of a 6-weight masquerading as a much lighter weight rod.

That illusion is not shattered when I join the rod sections and heft it. The rod gives me a different sense of where its gravity is located. The weight is out away from the butt, where I'm most accustomed to finding it on 6-weight rods. There is a pleasant sense of lightness. This feeling is what semihollow construction buys you in a 6-weight bamboo fly rod.

The lightness turns to grace when I rig up with a 6-weight double-taper fly line and give the rod a whirl on the lawn. It casts a delicate, sensitive line close-in and out to normal fishing ranges, but there is an undercurrent of restrained power in the rod.

A few false casts and a single haul have the double-taper 6-weight line gracefully winging out to 55 feet. A quick double haul adds 10 or 15 more feet. I can tell that this will be my rod for our medium to larger Rocky Mountain trout streams. In all honesty, it's delicate enough close-in for our small upland streams. It has all the advantages of a 5-weight rod in terms of lightness and control, but it has the heart of a 6-weight rod. I see it helping me to quickly land larger trout from my home water on Colorado's South Platte River and tangling with bruisers over on the Roaring Fork or up in Wyoming or Montana.

Eight months later, the replacement tip for the ill-fated "teething tip" has arrived. Jim called and said he'd beefed it up a bit and wanted my thoughts on it. Oh, mama. If the first tip was grace, this tip is power with grace. I was out double hauling it with a Wulff Long Belly 6-weight line, and it just romped. No other words for it. It single hauls, it double hauls, it roll casts, it casts small- to medium-sized bass bugs, it casts streamers, and it can present a #20 Parachute Adams quite nicely. It's the all-around 6-weight rod that I've longed for. I've decided to take it on an overnighter to Wenatchee, Washington, for a little belly boat fishing on a few glacially formed lakes that hold some very hot rainbow trout.

Shortly after my arrival in Wenatchee, my host Gary Anderson has me enthroned on a borrowed belly boat in the shallow arm of Dry Falls Lake. The lake is known for large midges, and Gary has come up with a sweet midge emerger pattern for catching them on top. This is a new, challenging kind of fishing for me. The idea is to cast the floating midge emerger pattern out and let it sit on the water's surface until the trout find it. It helps if you can put it near where you have spotted a fish, and that means you need to be able to read very subtle signs—like what Gary calls a flat spot on the water's surface—to locate the trout.

A longer cast is advantageous much of the time. The Hidy 6-weight with the long belly line is up to the challenge. As for me being up to the challenge of spotting subtly rising trout and the flat spots created by them on the water's surface, I'm working at it.

I land a few. Gary lands considerably more and kindly comments that it surprises him that an 8-foot rod casts so well from the belly boat. That's what happens when you come to the party with a snazzy date.

Before the trip to Washington ends, the Hidy 6-weight has landed trout from several prairie lakes and caught trout feeding selectively to a little #22 Pale Morning Dun hatch on a spring creek known as Rocky Ford. You can't ask for more.

September 2000. You should know that I have just headed back to my truck from the South Platte River in Colorado's South Park to exchange the 9-foot, 6-weight Payne that I was fishing for the 8-foot, 6-weight Hidy. I dearly love Payne rods. That should tell you how I feel about the Hidy.

CHAPTER FOUR

H. L. Jennings
Split-Bamboo
Fly Rods

December 1995. The first H. L. Jennings fly rod I ever saw was at the Angler's Covey in Colorado Springs, Colorado. Actually, there were two of them, both 7½-feet long: one for a 4-weight line, the other for a 5-weight. They were safely displayed in a glass case.

A Jennings rod is strikingly beautiful. The straw-colored cane crescendos from the tip to a handsomely swelled butt just above the cigar-shaped cork handle. The reel seat spacer is a finely figured piece of olive, tiger maple, or eucalyptus wood. The hardware is nickel silver with either a slide band or a screw lock. The Swiss-type ferrules are a distinctive 1× short. A ferrule plug fits snugly into the butt section ferrule for storage or transport. The hard chrome snake guides are wrapped with transparent honey lemon thread that exquisitely offsets the cane. Wraps often are tipped with a turn or two of camel- or rust-colored thread. The ferrules are wrapped brown with gold or camel tipping.

Homer Jennings

PHOTO BY ED ENGLE

Finally, there is the varnish. I think the Jennings varnish ranks right up there with the best. It's clear, bright, and beautiful.

Needless to say, seeing those Jennings rods under glass was not enough. Kent Brekke, then the owner of the Covey, suggested that rather than drooling over the case, I take one of the rods out to the lawn and cast it. I chose the 4-weight.

Every fly rod will cast line. Some do it begrudgingly, others fling or even launch the line out. But a very few bring the fly line to life. When I cast the Jennings, it made me feel as if the fly line wanted to race through the guides to its destination. I can't get enough of that kind of feeling.

Several years later, when I met Homer Jennings in Colorado Springs, I asked him what he likes in a cane fly rod.

"I like a rod that responds with delicacy, mind you, but with a little speed to it so a nice loop can be formed. It should load progressively so you can fish a short line if you have to, but still be able to use more of the rod as you increase the cast," he said.

I knew then that he was my kind of rodmaker.

Homer Jennings started building cane rods in the 1970s when he met an old-timer fishing a cane rod on a reservoir near Cambridge, England. It turns out that the Englishman built cane rods. Jennings visited him a number of times and began to learn the trade.

"I actually learned from several old-timers who'd been making rods for years. One of them had a grandfather who'd made rods, so it was kind of a family tradition," Jennings said.

Jennings, a Texan, settled in England, where he ran a guest house for sixteen years before returning to the United States in 1992.

"I always had a shop in the guest house where I built rods. Eventually, I bought some bamboo, a milling machine, and a couple of lathes from a father and son who were moving their rod-building business to Ireland. I got what they didn't want to pack," Jennings said.

Jennings said that English cane rods often differ from American cane rods in that they have heavy and cumbersome tips.

"The English idea of a strong rod meant a strong tip in many cases, but not all of them. Hardy made some lightweight rods that were sensitive and responsive. A lot of them were sent to the States, where the market demanded a lighter more delicate rod. The English still make some heavy-duty stuff. Some of those old salmon rods weighed a huge amount. You fish one of them all day and you know it," he said.

Jennings's own rods are decidedly sensitive and delicate, with some of his best work being done in shorter length, lighter line weight models.

"Those old heavy-tipped English rods were hell to fish in close. I think that's one of the great attributes of American rods. Most of them have fine tips and can be used for close-in work. Bamboo is perfect for this, too. It kind of loads itself. It loads much quicker than graphite because most graphite rods are just a stiff butt with a sort of wavy tip on it. You have to really struggle to get the line out on some of them," Jennings said.

Jennings uses planing forms and a milling machine to build rods.

"The milling machine is more of a production tool. You use it if you have to make a half dozen 7½-foot, 5-weight rods. If someone orders a single rod, it's often easier to hand plane it," he said.

Jennings designed his own milling machine and then had it built in England.

"If you set the milling machine up right, it can be incredibly accurate. It's really pretty high-tech, too. In a lot of cases you might even consider a properly set-up milling machine to be superior to hand planing because of the accuracy you can attain. You can produce six strips that are exactly the same. You can literally cut a piece of bamboo to the width of a gnat's ass," he said.

Jennings said the most tedious part of his job is straightening the nodes on the bamboo. He uses a variable paint-stripping heat gun to heat the bamboo and then bend it into useable form. Once the nodes are straightened and planed into strips, he glues them together to form the blank.

"I use the best glue you can get. It's the resin that's used to glue helicopter rotor blades together. It just doesn't fall apart," Jennings said.

In addition, he uses two different epoxies to attach the ferrules. The different epoxies expand when mixed, making a particularly strong bond. Epoxy is also used to finish the reel seat spacers. Several coats are applied, along with an ultraviolet inhibitor. The result is an extremely tough finish that is very resistant to scratching.

Jennings said that he's learned over the years what it takes to produce a good rod.

"You look at other rods and begin to see where yours fall short, especially when it comes to cosmetics. I'll see something I like and try to incorporate it in my rods. You're always learning about rod action, too, and how you think a rod should feel and what people like you to incorporate into your tapers. The swelled butt is a good example. I've found that I like it for more than just cosmetics. It really does seem to stop the action right above the thumb. I don't like the action to go down into the handle," he said.

I asked Homer what his current favorite rod is.

"It's a three-piece, 7½-foot for a 5-weight line. It's a beautiful little rod. It has a nice fast tip and can cast to 20 yards with no trouble at all, but it's so easy to fish in close with it, too. And it weighs only 3½ ounces. It's quite handy," he replied.

I can see him on the water with that rod now. He is probably working a trout that is busy sipping spent Trico spinners or porpoising to emerging midges. It is the kind of fishing that requires delicate, accurate casts. They are the kind of casts where the line must zip unobstructed and free through the guides. It's where the rod is charged with settling the fly perfectly on the water's surface.

I can see all of that. Homer Jennings makes a damn fine rod.

April 1997. If you're serious about bamboo, it has always been my belief that you should move to a town where a master rodmaker lives. It was my good fortune when I discovered Homer Jennings's work at the Angler's Covey and then found out that he lived nearby. Through a series of coincidences and some work I was doing on cane rods, Homer and I met and developed a friendship. It's all about bamboo, although we sometimes find time to rave about the government, blood pressure, and barking dogs. He is my man when I have questions about a rod, and over the years we've met many times to cast rods that have come my way.

Homer sees everything about a rod. He always peers down its length first to check for straightness, then looks at the quality of the bamboo itself, the node work, ferrule work, quality of cork in the grip, and hardware. Once in awhile he'll pick up a magnifying glass to closely examine some detail that only a rodmaker thinks about.

"I know I shouldn't be doing this," he apologizes as he peers through the glass, "but I just have to know. I guess I'm too critical. I just hope the other rodmakers are doing this to my rods, too. We're all quite alike, aren't we?"

Sooner or later we end up casting out on the lawn in front of his house.

He'll croon, "Oh, I like that," or ask, "Don't you think there's a bit of a dead spot above the ferrule?" or exclaim, "That one puts the line out!"

We've been going on like that for years now. After awhile we retire back to the kitchen, where there is usually a rod tip or midsection in the process of being wrapped. Homer moves them aside and asks, "How about a spot of tea?"

I drink my tea and think about how much I've learned.

August 2000. My sweetheart, Jana, wanted to get me something for a wedding gift when we were married last year. Without hesitation I suggested an H. L. Jennings split-cane fly rod. It has taken the better part of eight months to work through the waiting list and my standard agony of indecision over exactly which rod to get. I started off wanting a 7-weight rod. Homer mentioned he had a taper similar to a Payne that might work nicely on a 7-weight rod, and we left it at that until my mind started working overtime. After considerable machinations on my part, I decided that for this rod I wanted something that I would fish more often than a 7-weight. That led unequivocally to a 5-weight, which is the home water rod of choice for where I live.

After deciding on the line weight, the rest was relatively easy. I went with an 8-foot, three-piece rod. The three-piece rod has become crucial if you want to avoid checking it when flying. I debated the 8-foot length for awhile because I have a bit of a soft spot for 8½-foot rods. They make mending line just a little easier and can be graceful, elegant, and fun to cast. The downside is that in terms of rod design there isn't a lot to go on for an 8½-foot three-piece rod. There are plenty of two-piece 8½-footers and three-piece 9-footers. In contrast, three-piece 8-foot rods are common with well-known design characteristics. With all of that in mind, I opted for the 8-foot length, figuring that I'll just stretch my arm a little longer for some of the mends.

Besides, the 8-foot length meets what has become one of my more basic rod-buying criteria. I like to ask the rodmaker which of his rods he likes the most and which lengths and line weight models he most often makes. I like having a rod that most accurately represents the maker's work. It's actually a very practical consideration, too. I think that if a rodmaker has made a number of rods of a certain length and line weight, there is a better chance that he may impart a special, almost intangible knowledge to the rod. It's the knowledge born from the many almost mantralike repetitions that form the basis of rod making. It's where intuition takes over. And once in awhile it imparts a spirit to the rod that verges on soul.

And even if you don't believe in all the hocus-pocus surrounding the alchemy of making a bamboo fly rod, it certainly makes sense that practice makes perfect. Wouldn't you rather have the surgeon who'd performed the operation you need two hundred times over the one who'd performed it five times?

Eventually Homer calls up. He's working on the blank as we speak and needs to know what color wraps I want. In keeping with my philosophy of sticking to what best represents the rod-maker's work, I ask for Jennings's trademark tan wraps, tipped brown.

The rod is complete within a few weeks. It's everything I had hoped for. The straight nickel silver cap, sliding band, and reel seat check are deeply blued. The sliding band is unusual because it has a 4 percent internal taper.

"You can't get a swaged band in the U.S. This reel seat hardware is made by Shirl Maisey in the U.K. The internal taper prevents the binding that you often get when the band is just straight," Jennings said.

The olive wood reel seat spacer is exquisite. Jennings applies four coats of two-part epoxy to the wood. Each coat is sanded down before the next coat is applied. The final coat is then taken down and buffed to a deep glossed finish. The spacer itself is best described as "radiused" to accept the reel seat.

"The reel seat isn't really flattened or mortised. It's radiused like you'd do pearling with cutters on a piece of wood, except it's shaped in a form to fit the concave part of the reel foot. It has a smaller radius there than the rest of the spacer. The foot may not fit perfectly, but that's the idea," Jennings said.

The 6-inch cigar grip is made with 8-millimeter cork rings rather than the standard 1/2-inch rings.

"The 8-millimeter cork rings are pretty dense. I think those are the ones they use to make the bottom of a champagne stopper. They're dense to keep those nice bubbles from escaping. It's the best cork I can find, even though it's a little harder to put together. You need two of these rings to make a conventional ring, but if you do get an imperfection, it goes only 8 millimeters rather than a 1/2 inch," Jennings said.

The deeply blued cork check by Bailey Woods gives way to tan wraps tipped red and then brown. The rod is signed "H. L. Jennings." The number to the left of the signature indicates the rod's origin in consecutive order from rod number 1. My rod is number 499. The length of the rod and line weight designation appear to the right of the signature. The date below the rod number signifies the date when the first coat of varnish was applied to the rod. The signature wrap, which Jennings refers to as a "twirl-zle," is three or four wraps of tan thread tipped with a couple of wraps of brown.

The agate stripper is a beautiful cloudy white/honey color made by Mike McCoy and Daryl Whitehead. The deeply blued ferrules are 1× short Swiss style from Bailey Woods. Ferrule wraps are brown tipped red and brown. The ferrule plugs are cut off six-sided bamboo bits fitted with cork. The bronzed line guides and tip-top are "Snake Brand" by Mike McCoy. They beautifully accentuate the blond bamboo. The tip-top is wrapped in tan thread tipped red and brown.

"The wire in these guides is graduated to the ID of the snake. That means that the smaller the guide gets, the smaller the wire gets. A lot of guide makers don't bother to do this anymore," Jennings said.

The bamboo itself is blond. The three-and-three node work is smooth, short, and exceptional. Jennings jokes that the "super-select bamboo is roughed out on a mill and finished on a hand planing form and blessed by Buddhist monks to do no harm." The finish is Spar-Urethane made by Minwax.

"It's a yacht varnish. I used to use R–10 Varmore, which is the stuff Garrison used, but it's difficult to find now and the Spar-Urethane works just as well and I can find it. When it gets too thick, I retire it," Jennings said.

Jennings said that he initially experimented with English tapers when he started building rods in the United Kingdom, but that they simply weren't as refined as American tapers.

"The English rods weren't as fine tipped as American rods. They really weren't even compound tapers. Most of them were just straight tapers done on a milling machine. You couldn't adjust the tips or butts to suit your needs. It was whatever the machine pushed out you got—skinny on one end and big on the other. Most people now are aware that the rods require a bit more refinement to get the best results," he said.

Jennings said that his main influence has come from Payne, Garrison, and Dickerson tapers.

"Everyone sort of steals everyone else's basic tapers, but we tweak them a bit because not all of us have the same taste in how a rod should cast or how a rod should react in your hand," he said.

Jennings said that he initially had a lot of trouble with three-piece rods. They seemed too slow because the midsection wasn't stiff enough.

"I had to work out the midsection for my three-piece rods myself on account of the problems I had with the speed of the rod. Garrison actually described in his book that you had to have an oversized midsection to get the right sort of feel in a three-piece rod. Getting it right is a hit-or-miss proposition. You just have to keep trying until you stumble on to it," he said.

Jennings said that he had come across some rods that had an enormous difference between the tip and the midsection.

"The tip was just kind of flopping around and the mid was stiff as a poker. That didn't accomplish what I needed, so I just kept refining it until I could accept the speed of the rod and have the least possible change from the tip to the butt, which keeps the tip from doing all the work," he said.

September 2000. John Gierach and I are camped on the Frying Pan River, as is our habit in September. We're the only two from our gang of pals who made the annual trip this year. I've brought the Jennings rod. I can't think of a better place to fish cane. There will be blue-winged olive hatches, sulfur hatches, midges, a few lingering green drakes, caddis, and possibly the enigmatic flightless *Serratella* mayfly.

There is a pool formed below an island. At the head it is "riffly" and rough. The main channel cuts along the opposite bank, but it is far enough out that there is a narrow slick between the channel and the shore. The rest of the pool is a gentle knee-deep riffle. We have seen trout rise in every square foot of it. This afternoon they are coming up most consistently to a little #24 blue-winged olive, but there are a few sulfurs sputtering off here and there.

I slip into the water at the tail of the pool. I've knotted a #24 Cul de Canard (CDC) blue-winged olive imitation to the tippet. There are trout steadily working in the slack water away from the main channel. The rises are the confident, almost languid kind, indicating that either the trout are taking bugs that cannot get away or there are so many bugs that they can go about their business unhurried.

I have cast the Jennings before and know that it feels good in the hand. The fly line seems to want to fly; the loops are smooth as silk, with no shockiness. But this is the first real test. Trout feeding on top in the slack water to tiny mayflies.

I like the feel of the rod when I false cast. It's oily smooth. I've felt that before, but what is more unusual and most impressive is how the fly goes directly to where it is aimed. I'm convinced that this accuracy is due in part to Homer's fastidiousness about his rods being absolutely straight. For close to flawless accuracy, I hold the rod straight up where I can sight it in close to my eye. The rest is intuition. That's what I like about it. The rod seems to act on my intuition. The fly is where I think it should be. And a trout comes up without hesitation to take it.

I look for rods that feel like an extension of my body, and for this hatch on this river this day the Jennings rod and I are one. I like that very much.

A little later John says, "That thing sure casts a nice loop."

Oh, mama.

CHAPTER FIVE

J. E. Arguello
Rod Company

May 1998. Joe Arguello and I are sitting in the Double Tree Restaurant in Platteville, Colorado, enjoying the afterglow of our first couple of bites into the rather large steak sandwiches that we've both ordered. Platteville is in eastern Colorado on the high plains. It's the other Colorado that you don't hear much about. The restaurant is nine miles north of Joe's home and rod-building shop in Ft. Lupton, Colorado, but he couldn't resist introducing me to it. It's real good food.

"This is farm country out here, and they just can't get away with serving bad beef," Joe says as he takes another bite.

Upon reflection, which I try not to do in the middle of a power lunch, it occurs to me that the quality of the beef at the Double Tree is very much like the state of bamboo rod building in the United States right now. If you are going to try to make a full-time living at building cane rods, you darn well better not build a bad one. The word will get around too quickly.

Joe Arguello

PHOTO BY ED ENGLE

As much as I like reminiscing about the golden age of bamboo fly rod building and the legendary and superb rods built by masters such as Payne, Leonard, Gillum, Garrison, and Dickerson, to name a few, I've become increasingly convinced that the golden age of the cane rod is right now. The quality of handcrafted cane rods being built today, in terms of both cosmetics and function, is unsurpassed. It only stands to reason, too, because these rods are being built on the firm foundation laid by the great craftsmen of the past.

Before lunch I'd spent the better part of the morning in Joe's shop and out on the lawn by his house casting examples of his craftsmanship.

Joe Arguello is a relatively new name to the ranks of full-time cane rodmakers. My friend John Gierach had called me a few weeks prior to my visit and casually asked, "Do you know about Joe Arguello out in Ft. Lupton?"

The implied message was that if I didn't know who Joe was it would behoove me to find out. As it turns out, I had heard about what was going on out in the other Colorado.

"I started building rods in 1992. My main influence was Mike Clark up in Lyons. I'd been to his shop and seen the work he was doing, and I just thought to myself that maybe I could do that, too," Arguello said.

Arguello got hold of the book *A Master's Guide to Building a Bamboo Fly Rod*, by Everett Garrison with Hoagy Carmichael, and went through it page by page. He augmented what he learned from Garrison with a copy of Wayne Cattanach's *Handcrafting Bamboo Fly Rods*.

"I'm essentially self-taught if that means I mainly used the books to learn by. They were my teachers," Arguello said.

It's apparent when you walk into Arguello's shop that he brings a very strong mechanical aptitude to his rod building. Lathes, drills, grinders, and a variety of other machines line the walls. He hand built the heat-treating oven for the cane, along with his planing forms. The fact is that Arguello has machined 90 percent of the tools he uses to build cane rods. A natural assumption would be that he would have a bevelling machine, but that is not the case.

"I do all the work on the planing forms," Arguello said.

Arguello's first shop, known as Rocky Mountain Cane, in Lafayette, Colorado, was a combination rod-building/fly-fishing store.

"It was open to the public, and every time I got going on wrapping a rod back in the shop, someone would come into the store and I'd have to break away and help them. I eventually realized that what I really wanted to do was just build cane rods.

That's when I closed the store and moved the shop into my house. My wife was gracious enough to allow me to cut a hole in the floor so I could drop my dip tank down into the basement," Arguello said.

Like most accomplished rod builders, Arguello can build a rod to the customer's specifications, but much of his work centers around his Garrison/Cattanach studies.

"A lot of my tapers are based on Garrison or Cattanach tapers. I don't really see a need to develop a new taper if for no other reason than to say it's mine. I might fiddle with a taper a little, but basically these tapers have stood the test of time," Arguello said.

Arguello's rods typically employ two-by-two node staggering, where a node is matched to one other node with two clear splines of bamboo between them. The next set of two nodes up the rod is placed one spline over, creating a spiral of matched nodes separated by two clear splines up the length of the rod.

"I'm big into heat treating, which shouldn't be confused with flaming. It dries the moisture and makes the blank a bit stiffer. Some kind of magical chemical change takes place. I don't know what it is, but I just like it," Arguello said.

Arguello prefers not to flame a blank, but he will on customer request. He does use ammonia in the heat-treating process to obtain a light wheat-colored blank.

"I work very hard when I glue the strips together. I want absolutely no glue lines. I'll trash a blank if I see a glue line," Arguello said.

Arguello's preferred reel seat is the hooded cap with sliding band. The hardwood insert is round. A cork check is used at the rear of the grip, along with a winding check up front. In addition to the hooded butt cap configuration, he also utilizes round butt caps with a flattened wood insert. The hardware is nickel silver. Although Arguello offers a number of grip options on his order blank, his own taste goes toward the classic cigar grip.

Arguello's rods are characteristically wrapped in traditional colors, such as tans, browns, and olives. If any tipping is used, it's usually just a few subdued windings. The result is a restrained, elegant appearance. The rods are signed "J. E. Arguello," with the rod length and recommended double-taper fly line weight and serial number below. The four-digit serial number designates the last two digits of the year the rod was built, followed by a two-digit number signifying the numerical order in which the rod was built. The serial number 9801 indicates the first rod built in 1998.

On basic rod models Arguello uses commercially available components, which include a carbide stripping guide, Super-Z-type ferrules, and sliding band reel seat. Arguello modifies the serrations on the ferrule by filing them to a point to prevent cracks in the varnish over the ferrule wraps. Wraps on basic models are one color. The marine spar varnish finish on the Arguello rod is immaculate.

"If a speck of dust shows up in the varnish, it gets sanded down and recoated. That's what the customer sees. I want it to be perfect," Arguello said.

What really sets Arguello apart from other rodmakers are his offerings above and beyond his basic model rod. Arguello is the only builder I know of at this time who will hand build every component of the fly rod upon customer request.

He has built a special set of tools to hand twist the reverse, or English-style, snake guides out of piano wire, which he then heat treats for color and hardness.

"I really like the English-style guide. It's more compressed than a regular snake guide. It just looks good," Arguello said.

He also handcrafts his own agate stripping guides. He makes the nickel silver frames and bezels. The agate is cut by hand and polished.

"I wanted to use agate stripping guides, but I found that the ones that were available always seemed to be too big or too small.

I decided to take a lapidary course to learn to cut the stone, and then I developed my own design for the frame and bezel. These stripping guides are functionally correct for modern fly lines," Arguello said.

Arguello's handmade reel seats are modeled after Garrison designs, which include a hooded butt cap, a swaged, checkered sliding band, and a checkered cork check. The hardwood insert is round.

Ferrules are modeled after the famous Super-Z and machined from nickel silver.

When we were done in the shop, Joe gathered up an armload of rod tubes and we retired to the lawn around his home on a quiet cul-de-sac.

"It's okay to just cast out on the pavement," he said as he began putting rods together.

He then handed me a nifty little two-piece 7-foot, 3-weight rod based on a Garrison 201E to begin with. My first test, as always, was to get a few feet of fly line out from the tip-top guide to see how the rod cast the leader. It passed admirably. I then proceeded to get 25 or 30 feet of the double-taper 3-weight line into the air. The rod false cast it smoothly with the characteristic Garrison-type feel. It's important to slow the rod a bit when casting to prevent overpowering it. This allows it to perform its magic. It's a sensuous taper to cast.

I cast the rod effortlessly to 50 feet, which is well beyond the range I would fish it. I suspect that if I'd chosen to crank down on it I might have coaxed 20 or more feet out, but I didn't see the point. I'm a fisherman, and I look for what a rod will do within the framework of how I would fish it. And I saw this rod as a pleasant companion for Colorado's sweet little upland streams, where a 25-foot cast is long. Besides, being the promiscuous rod aficionado that I am, I could not wait to get my hands on the two-piece 7½-foot, 4-weight that Joe was casting.

This was one of Arguello's totally hand-built rods. Before I cast it, I took a moment to admire all the fine work. The reel seat was exquisite, as was the handmade stripping guide. The English-style snake guides really are sexy. In the hand, the 4-weight, which was modeled on a Wayne Cattanach taper, somehow felt stronger, or perhaps I should say stouter, than many 4-weights I've held. It cast very well close-in, but the big surprise was what it did at longer distances. The rod never hesitated as I false cast more and more line into the air. With a little work, and when I got my timing dialed in, it was not difficult to cast close to the entire length of the fly line. It was a surprising performance for a 4-weight, especially in light of its excellent close-in casting capabilities.

I was getting a little giddy when Joe tapped me on the shoulder and stuck a 7-foot 9-inch three-piece for a 5-weight line based on a Garrison 209E taper in my hand. I had to tuck my elbow in a little on this rod and let it do more of the work, but when I did, the loops went out without a hint of shock waves. It was a delight to cast and performed nicely close-in, but the rod also had a core power, which I discovered when I lengthened the false casts and went for a bit of distance. My immediate thought was that the rod would make a fine all-around Rocky Mountain dry fly rod.

"I really like the 7-foot 9-inch length in a cane rod," Arguello commented. "I'm not sure why, but I think that 3-inch difference from 8 feet makes a difference."

As we were breaking the rods down and putting them back into the tubes, Joe dashed into the house and came out with just one more rod.

"You shouldn't leave without casting this," he said, while he put together a two-piece 6-footer for a 4-weight.

It was an amazing rod close-in. I've had a number of discussions with other fly fishers on how to describe casting accuracy in rods and for the most part have come to the conclusion that accuracy is more a function of the caster than the rod, but I also feel that a rod can make it easier for a caster to be accurate. That's how I felt about the little 6-footer. It just seemed to want to go where I pointed it.

On top of the wonderful feel and close-in accuracy of the rod, which is based on a Cattanach taper, it was pleasant to cast at medium and some quite long distances. It responded very well to the double haul, which can only be a plus in shorter rod lengths when distance is required.

Sometime during the day Joe had made a comment that came to mind as I was hurtling through Denver in an attempt to beat the four o'clock urban rush hour.

"The bamboo limits you in a number of ways, and the best thing I think you can do is to just craft it as well as you can. I was an auto body repairman for twenty years, and I worked to the same standard. They just wanted production work—get the cars in and get them out. Now, with the bamboo, I can be as precise and caring as I want, instead of just saying it's good enough for the insurance company that's footing the bill. That's why I do this," he said.

If you're ever around Ft. Lupton and get a chance, you might try test casting one of the rods that is a result of that precision and caring. And while you're at it, the steak sandwiches aren't too bad up at the Double Tree in Platteville.

July 1998. Joe Arguello, Chuck McGuire, John Gierach, and I are in Colorado's North Park. We are all bamboo rod aficionados, and we've come to the North Fork of the North Platte River with a pretty impressive array of lumber.

For myself I've packed Joe's fine 7-foot 9-inch rod for a 5-weight line that is built along the lines of the Garrison 209E; the 8-foot, 5-weight Cutthroat Special that Mike Clark made for me several years ago; an old Wright McGill Granger Special; and a 9-foot Phillipson Power Pakt. I didn't realize when I put the selection together that all these cane rods were built in Colorado by Colorado rodmakers. It seems appropriate upon reflection.

I like North Park partly because it reminds me of the Colorado I moved to close to thirty years ago. I don't know if it's the last best place in Colorado, but it does reflect the more rural ranching lifestyle that I remember once dominated much of the state. I do know that I'm in love with the rivers of North Park. The North Platte River, the Michigan River, the Illinois River, the Roaring Fork River, and the North Fork of the North Platte all meander through the hay fields in the broad valley. And they are something to look at.

As much as I like the beauty of the valley and fishing with cane rods, there is one thing I like more and that is the wild brown trout that live in those rivers. They can be difficult and temperamental, or on the best days, they can provide the kind of dry fly angling that I dream about.

We are guests at the recently opened Old Boettcher Lodge on privately held water on the North Fork of the North Platte River. It is a wonderful, luxurious place and is one of several ways to go in North Park, which is just now beginning to open up to its fly-fishing potential. I should also say that I have fished many of the public leases in North Park and the brown trout are there, too, also rising to dry flies on the good days.

Our first two days on the North Fork have been marked by heavy rain and high water. We've managed to pound up a few fish on larger attractor dry flies, but the water has clearly put the fish off.

I resorted to a Woolly Bugger fished streamer style with the Cut-throat Special for awhile and found that the brown trout were not entirely off the feed. Many were riding the pressure waves in front of the grassy protrusions that jut out into the river. Some were backed up in the quiet water in the bends. Most averaged around 12 or 14 inches, but a few measured to 17 inches and were deep.

But that has all changed today. Bob Wills, the head guide at the Old Boettcher Lodge, said that the water would go down as fast as it came up, and true to his word, the river has cleared and dropped almost a foot today. The air is full of #16 pale morning duns and a larger mayfly known as a flav, which is short for *Ephemerella flavilinea*. It's a latinized way of saying that the bug is a somewhat smaller rendition of the Western Green Drake. And all Colorado fly fishers hold the Western Green Drake in reverence —as do the brown trout.

I have broken out Joe's rod for the day's fishing. More than anything I like the oily smooth way the rod casts a fly line. Casting at standard fishing ranges is effortless. There are no shock waves in the loop, and I'm able to put the fly exactly where I want it to go. I'm fishing a short bend in the river with an overhanging willow toward the tail. Trout are rising all over it.

I started by casting a #12 Gray Wulff to the easier fish rising in the shallow water out from the cut bank. They are nice brown trout. Some go to 14 inches. I have noticed that the spots on these brown trout seem to be arranged more conservatively than on other brown trout I have caught in Colorado. They are a bit farther apart and may be a little larger than they are on South Platte River browns. They remind me of the native brown trout in Ireland. I wonder if they might be a purer strain of brown trout that have managed to survive in North Park from their original stocking without the help of additional plantings.

But all of that aside, there is a very nice fish rising directly in front of the willow that sweeps out into the current. I know that I will have to try this fish, and the risks are obvious. A misplaced cast will end up in the willow. An uncontrolled drift will tangle.

It's the ideal situation for a fancy cast known as the right-hand curve, and this is the ideal fly rod to pull it off. A properly executed curve will put the fly right where it must be for the trout to take it. It entails overpowering things a bit to get the fly to flick over to the right. I don't consciously think about doing any of the fancy stuff when I'm false casting, but rather just think about getting the fly to the trout. When I let the cast go, it is perfect and the trout rises without hesitation to take it.

It's a large fish and I do what I can to move it out into the main current and away from the willow and the undercut banks. I'm very quickly forced to follow it downstream and briefly worry about all that can go wrong. But for once, things go according to plan. I manage to net and release an 18-inch wild brown trout. I caught it on the one cast in a million that goes perfectly. The spots on the fish are gorgeous.

It's a good time to sit down by the North Fork of the North Platte River and look up at the sky. I don't know how it is that one fly rod becomes a favorite, but I have a sense that this is the beginning of a long friendship.

June 1999. I've just heard that Joe has moved, taken a job, and is still making fly rods on the side. That's good news—that he's still making rods. Making bamboo fly rods full-time is not an easy row to hoe. It really is a labor of love. I think Joe will tell you that, and he might mention that if you're ever in Platteville, you might still want to check out the steak sandwiches.

April 2001. Joe Arguello is making a very limited number of rods at this time. He told me that he never got quite the number of orders that he needed to keep at it full-time.

"You never know, though. I could get some time and get back into it down the road. That's why I still try to keep my name out there just a little. I love building the rods, but right now I'm pretty much just fishing and that's not too bad," Joe said.

Joe said he's still interested in hearing from anyone interested in an Arguello bamboo fly rod. "We can talk and just see where it goes from there," he said.

CHAPTER SIX

J. D. Wagner
Rods

December 1997. The first thing you notice when you uncase one of Jeff Wagner's rods is the finish. The varnish is exquisite. It gives the cane a depth and clarity that is unusual even in this day of increasingly finely crafted and finished bamboo rods. And as much as Wagner might urge you to critically examine the work because "no rod is perfect," it is difficult to find flaws.

"I go to a lot of work to make the varnish look the way it does, but in terms of absolute functionality you could probably dip a rod with one coat and it would be sealed just fine. That rod would probably function well and hold up just as long, but building a good rod means attending to the details. Rod builders are held to higher standards now. Rods not only have to be functional, they almost have to be works of art," Wagner said.

Jeff Wagner brightened an otherwise somber and wintry December week when he shipped me three rods to take a look at.

Casimira Orlowski and Jeff Wagner

The rods represented a broad range of Wagner's considerable talent. There was a three-piece 6-foot 3-inch, 4-weight that packs down to a 25-inch length; a three-piece 8-foot, 4- or 5- weight; and an exquisitely crafted limited edition rod whose inspiration was taken from the limited edition Thomas & Thomas Fountainhead that was produced in 1983.

I began my now standard lawn tests with the 6-foot 3-inch, 4-weight. Wagner designates it a Model 363-M, which stands for three pieces 6 feet 3 inches. The alpha designation is for Wagner's use in the shop. It's a classic small-stream rod that might best be applied to those wonderfully intimate small waters that may be no wider than 10 feet or so. The taper is broadly based on the legendary Paul Young Midge, but Wagner has lightened up the tip a bit. You'll notice this immediately when you work the rod close-in.

Although casting a standard 7½-foot to 9-foot small-stream leader with a rod this length can be difficult, the Model 363-M does very well, with as little as a foot or so of a 4-weight double-taper line extended out past the tip-top. That's as good as any short rod that I've cast in awhile. The rod casts with ease at typical small-stream operating distances out to about 45 feet. The action is quick but not overly fast. The rod is light and capable of the delicate sort of presentations so often required on small streams. Surprisingly, it also has a strong backbone. If you decide you need to cast a fly with a 6-foot 3-inch rod into the next county, the Model 363-M will get you the first 70 to 75 feet of that distance with little more than the tug of a single haul. In more adept hands than mine, I think it could be cast to quite long distances.

The cane on the Model 363-M, like all of Wagner's rods, is flamed to a fine medium brown/gold tone. Nodes on Wagner's rods are staggered traditionally with a three-on-three arrangement. The node work is flat, smooth, and short, demonstrating that some time and care were taken in straightening and working with the cane.

The all-cork grip and spacer is a modified cigar shape. The total length is 8 inches, with the grip itself measuring around 5 inches. The REC nickel silver reel seat hardware consists of a pocketed butt cap with sliding ring. The winding check is a nickel silver Bellinger. The rod has a unique hook keeper.

"I have a friend locally who dabbles in cane rod building and jewelry making. He makes a unique sterling silver rope braid ring hook keeper that I use on my rods," Wagner said.

The line guides on the Model 363-M are wrapped in translucent silk tipped black, giving the rod a nicely understated look. At the Super Swiss ferrules, which are standard on Wagner rods, the wraps are black. You will also note a band of varnish on the ferrule above the black wrap. Wagner retains this feature when he removes the protective tape from around the ferrules after the varnish-dipping operation. The band of varnish is straightened with a razor when the tape is removed.

The stripping guide is a Daryll Whitehead agate in a nickel silver frame. Snake guides are from Pacific Bay. Wagner takes care to polish the feet of the guides before winding the wraps.

The placement of line guides on Wagner's rods may surprise some aficionados. On the Model 363-M the stripper is rather close to the handle.

"When I come up with a rod design, I shift line guides around and add guides until I think the rod casts best. I don't really stand on convention when it comes to guides. On the 6-foot 3-inch rod, discerning people will notice right off that the stripping guide is way back, but it's there for only one reason. It makes the rod cast better," Wagner said.

I might also mention that the Model 363-M, along with all of Wagner's rods at the time of this writing, comes in a finely crafted matching six-sided wood case of either curly maple or walnut.

Switching over to casting Wagner's three-piece 8-foot Model 380 TNS for a 4- or 5-weight double-taper line from the Model 363-M was an exciting change. Where the Model 363-M action is quick to suit the kind of small-stream pocket water fishing where it's used, the Model 380 TNS casts in a stately, mellow, relaxed manner. The medium action is ideal for delicate dry fly presentations. Once again Wagner has modified a classic taper, in this case an F. E. Thomas design, to come up with a taper uniquely suited for modern cane rods.

This rod bucks a current idea among cane rod enthusiasts that dry fly action equals fast action. It's an idea that's come from the increasing use of graphitelike rod tapers on cane rods. The reason for the trend is obvious when you consider that many fly fishers come to bamboo from graphite and a faster action cane rod is easier for them to adjust to. Cane rod builders will tell you that it's easier to sell a fast action nowadays, and that's a shame. I am a great fan of medium dry fly action. It's because I cast medium action better, and I believe these actions are capable of great delicacy when properly cast.

As I look through Wagner's list of available tapers, I like the idea that he'll stick his neck out and produce some fine medium-action rods. The Paul Young influence can be strongly seen in modified Para-15 and Para-17 designs, along with Paul Young Midge, Driggs, and Princess spin-offs. There's also some quicker action Payne-like designs and a Granger-like design.

"I've found that the faster action rods are the easiest for me to sell, but it's my personal feeling that you have to build some rods that are a little different from what everyone else is doing. And right now the trend is toward faster Garrison-like tapers because they are readily available to rod builders who are just starting out," Wagner said.

He's also the first to point out a fact that many rod builders don't want to admit about tapers.

"I am very up-front about tapers. Whenever I give a presentation or demonstrate my rods at a show, I tell people I get my tapers the old-fashioned way. I steal them. That means I like to start with established tapers from a variety of makers, such as Payne, Young, or F. E. Thomas, and tweak them a little to meet my needs. I lightened up the tip of the Model 363-M quite a bit so it would cast better close-in. But the bottom line is that there seems to be a set number of basic foundation tapers that work well, and we all use them as a base for our modifications," Wagner said.

The Model 380 TNS is a sweet casting rod. It takes just a moment to realize that you must slow down your casting stroke a bit to let this rod do its work. Once you click into the proper timing, you'll feel the action move down toward the butt of the rod as more line is false cast out. The rod casts easily to 55 or 60 feet, and with the addition of a single or double haul, you can effortlessly lengthen out to around 75 feet as long as you take care to not over-power it. Where you go beyond that depends on your technique.

Length of casts aside, I see the 380 TNS more as a medium-range rod that is capable of delivering delicate dry fly presenta-tions. This is a rod that demonstrates the great variety of actions that are available in cane. If you come to it from graphite, you'll probably find that your timing is off in the beginning, but if you stick with the rod, you'll realize that dry fly action doesn't have to be tippy and fast—it can also be relaxed, delicate, and stately. Somewhat more-experienced cane rod enthusiasts will immedi-ately appreciate the 380 TNS.

The 380 TNS is fitted with a western grip. The reel seat is a nickel silver uplocking Bob Venneri screw lock with an impreg-nated maple burl insert.

"I like the impregnated wood because it's beautiful and holds up. Varnished spacers tend to get dinged over time, and the varnish chips and wears. The impregnated spacer always looks like new. If you look closely, you'll see that the colors of maple that I use har-monize well with the color in the cane. You'll also see that the knurled winding check matches the knurling on the end cap. These are just some little things, but when you put them together you can achieve a pleasing harmony," Wagner said.

The other details on the Model 380 TNS match those on the Model 363-M. Line guide wraps are translucent silk tipped black, the hook keeper is a sterling silver rope braid ring, the ferrules are Super Swiss, and the stripping guide is agate.

The final rod Jeff Wagner sent me is a dazzler. It's the sort of work that rodmakers do once in awhile just to stretch out a little and try new techniques. Most often you'll hear this kind of work described as presentation rods or limited edition rods. This was Wagner's 1997 Limited Edition Rod.

"I'd call this a limited edition sort of thing. Each year I'm going to make a very small number of rods that in some way will challenge my skills as a craftsman in order for me to grow technically and as an artist," Wagner said.

Wagner said the inspiration for his 1997 Limited Edition Rod was taken from the Thomas & Thomas Fountainhead, which was a limited edition rod produced in 1983.

The defining characteristic of the Fountainhead, which imitates rods built at the turn of the century, occurs in the butt section. Walnut or a similar wood is spliced into the cane to form a dramatic swell and then continued to form an all-wood-and-cane grip and reel seat as well.

Wagner's three-piece 8-foot rendition features a REC nickel silver pocketed butt cap with sliding band. A knurled ring at the forward portion of the spliced walnut and cane reel seat acts as a reel seat check. The end of the spliced walnut-and-cane grip is designated by another ring that visually designates the end of the handle and the start of the swell. Light olive intermediate wraps then proceed to an agate stripping guide, which is wrapped in light olive. The ferrules are Super Swiss and wrapped in dark olive. The line guides are wrapped in light olive. The light olive wraps at the tip-tops are tipped in red.

The overall effect of the rod is astounding. The workmanship at the grip and reel seat where the walnut and cane is spliced is immaculate. Top that with the incomparable Wagner spar varnish finish, and you indeed have a dazzling fly rod.

"During the building process, I learned a lot. This splicing isn't a new idea. If you look at rods built before 1900, you'll notice that many had spliced strips just forward of the grip that produced a dramatic swell. Typically they were made with blond cane and a cedar insert. You'll also see it in some other Thomas &

Thomas special edition and limited edition rods, such as the Just Swell, which had the splice before the grip, and the Fountainhead, which had the full splice all the way back into the reel seat," Wagner said.

Wagner said that the challenge was to figure out how the splicing was done and then proceed to design the tools he needed to do it.

"Interestingly enough, I noticed that the splicing was a feature on some old-production rods as well as on fancier rods. That made me think that it might not be a super difficult thing to do. They must have been able to do it quickly. So my challenge was to figure out how to do it efficiently. It took a lot of time to get everything just right," Wagner said.

A single example of some of the difficulties in building the rod was that Wagner had to build a larger dip tube to be able to varnish the wider handle on the rod. He also found that when he got the rod three-quarters down into the tube it floated and bobbed like a cork. That meant he had to devise a way to weight the rod in the dip tube. He ended up dipping the grip and then turning the rod over to dip the reel seat barrel to prevent getting varnish on the grip check.

The final result is a stunningly gorgeous rod. And you can count on one hand the rod builders capable of crafting it.

Wagner said that his next limited edition rod may feature a swell with a different type of wood and perhaps a rattan grip.

"Now that I have the swell figured out I can take off in a lot of different directions," he said.

These three rods show as broad a range of craftsmanship in the art of split-cane rod building as I've seen. It's also encouraging to see a rod builder working with some of the classic medium-action tapers that complement bamboo so well.

The beauty of the cane rod is that it is capable of handling so many tapers and actions. There is no single action that describes it. Jeff Wagner's work demonstrates that variety.

April 1998. Jeff Wagner mentioned that he has come out with a no-frills, economically priced line of split-cane fly rods. The two-piece single-tip rods are built with flamed cane. The nickel silver butt cap, slide band, and ferrules are oxidized. The stripper guide is by Mildrum, and the snake guides are chrome. The finish is a low-maintenance hand-rubbed penetrating polymer. Guide wraps are sienna brown. The rod comes complete with cloth bag and aluminum case.

The rods, known as the Patriot Series, come in three models: a 6-foot 3-inch for a 3- or 4-weight line; a 7-foot 3-inch for a 4- or 5-weight line, and a 7-foot 9-inch for a 5- or 6-weight line.

The Patriot Series rods are a reasonably priced introduction to the world of bamboo fly rods for those new to cane.

March 2001. Over the years, Jeff Wagner and I have kept up the friendly and sometimes cynical banter that self-employed people who work at home alone engage in. I call him every three or four months, and we rave about what's new. Maybe it's the fact that Wagner is now using Venneri hardware or the price of glue is up or the blue-winged olive hatch is on. Sometimes we talk about the real costs of working for yourself and wonder if it's worth it. We always end up deciding that it is indeed the good life. Our mutual salutation for when we hang up has become, "Keep living the dream, brother."

Although making high-quality split-cane fly rods continues to be the primary focus for Wagner, he has expanded his business to include teaching several six-day bamboo rod-making classes a year and selling of rod-building tools, supplies, and components.

More importantly, Jeff's partner, Casimira Orlowski, came on as a full-time rodmaker three years ago.

"She's the only full-time female cane rod builder anywhere in the world. We work together, side by side, much as the Dettes did," Jeff said.

"I kept working as a hospital administrator when Jeff went into full-time rod building six years ago. I had no intention of building rods then, but I didn't like my job that much either. After twenty years I was tired of the politics of hospitals. I was always behind a desk dealing with people. At the end of the day, I never could show anything concrete that I'd made. I'd always wanted to make things, and I'd had an interest in carpentry, too. So, I was planning to make a change at the time. I just wasn't sure what I'd do," Casimira said.

She said that her reasons for eventually getting into rod building were mostly practical.

"I really wanted to be self-employed, and I wanted to build something. I figured that building cane rods meets those requirements, and I do fish, so I appreciated the rods. I also realized that it was hard enough financially for us to start the one business. Starting another would be a real strain, so I became a rod builder," she said.

Casimira said that Jeff and she typically split up the rod-making chores. She likes pulling the bamboo culms and doing the preliminary work like splitting, flaming, and straightening and dressing nodes.

"I enjoy varnishing, too, because that's when the rod really becomes very beautiful, but it's a tricky part of the process. So sometimes it's enjoyable and sometimes it's not. The only thing that I don't do is wraps. Jeff has real steady hands and he's just so much better than me, so I don't do wraps," she said.

Casimira said that after she does the preliminary work Jeff often mills the strips and does some hand planing. The two of them then glue the strips together, and whoever has the time sands them after the glue has dried.

Casimira said that among the rod models they offer, the two-piece single-tip Patriot rods that they introduced several years ago have done well.

"When we came out with the Patriots, we were concerned that they would take away from our Signature series rods. We didn't want that to happen because the Signature rods are challenging and beautiful to make. As it turns out, the Patriot series has found its own little niche and not affected the Signature rod sales at all. We find that the Patriots sell well in retail settings. A lot of anglers are interested in the Patriots as kind of an entry to bamboo rods," she said.

Casimira said that making the Patriot rods is nice because the strips of bamboo leftover when a two-tip rod is made can be utilized to make the Patriot rods.

"It's nice for us because when you split bamboo, if everything goes perfectly, you'll get two rods out of a culm. The catch is that something usually goes wrong when you're straightening a section or whatever. Our tips for our two-piece and three-piece two-tip rods are all mirror matched, so we sometimes end up with an extra strip. The Patriots are a nice answer to what to do with those extra strips," she said.

Casimira said that it's interesting how getting into full-time rod building has gradually taken over their home.

"Our shop is a large garage that we converted, but it didn't stop there. We have a split-level home, and the lower level has ended up an office and varnishing area. Our smallest bedroom is dedicated to rod wrapping and the varnishing of rod wraps. We keep it a little warmer and the door is always closed to keep the dust down," she said.

It's clear when talking with Casimira and Jeff that they have dedicated themselves to the craft of rod building. But the real proof is in their work—from the flawless Presentation rods to the ideal fishing characteristics of their Signature rods to the wonderful practicality of the Patriot series.

Look for these rods to be around for a long time.

CHAPTER SEVEN

The Jenkins Rod Company

IT'S A BRISK FEBRUARY AFTERNOON IN DENVER, 1996. THE temperature at the snow-covered school yard where I'm casting is about five degrees below zero. It's not the kind of situation that even the most ardent cane rod enthusiast would choose to endure. But today is different. I'm in the school yard with Charlie Jenkins and his son Steven. And we are casting the incomparable Jenkins rod.

Jenkins bamboo fly rods earned their reputation for excellence on the difficult waters of Colorado's South Platte River in the renowned Cheeseman Canyon. Charlie, who was a tool planner and inspector in Denver's aerospace industry, fished the canyon often in the late 1950s. His dedication to fly-fishing and interest in tools and tool making naturally led him to rod building.

"I'd built one rod, and it turns out that Jim Poor, who was a huge influence on fly fishing in Denver, liked it a lot. He never

Charlie Jenkins and his son Steven.

told me that, but his wife came by one day and asked if she could buy it for him for his birthday. I said sure, but I told her I didn't know if it would hang together," Charlie said.

Apparently the rod did hang together and Poor, who owned the Mountain View Tackle Shop (later known as Angler's All) in Denver, started showing it off to other fly fishermen.

"The next thing I know he's selling them. I was in business before I knew it. They sold for $47.50! Neither of us was making any money, but the word got out," Charlie said.

The first Jenkins rods were 7½ feet of oven-tempered cane for a 5-weight line.

"These rods evolved around a group of serious fly fishermen who spent a lot of their time in Cheeseman Canyon. Most of them were not trying to reach far, but they had to have good presentation, so the rods were built for casting in a 30- to 35-foot range. But that doesn't mean they won't go farther. I didn't build anything but 5-weight rods for a long time because that's what these guys asked for," Charlie said.

Word about the Jenkins rod spread throughout the West. Dan Bailey said it was the best rod he ever carried at his Livingston, Montana, fly shop.

"You didn't buy Dan Bailey's approval, so I was very proud when he sent me a letter saying my rods were the best rods they ever carried," Charlie said.

The reputation of the rod eventually made its way throughout the United States and to Europe and Japan.

Charlie continued building rods through the 1960s and 1970s. Although Jenkins would make whatever kind of rod a customer ordered, he began concentrating on four standard rod styles that typified his ideas about cane rod construction. The standard line consisted of a 7-foot for a 3- or 4-weight line, a 7-foot for a 4- or 5- weight line, a $7^1/_2$-foot for a 4- or 5-weight line, and an 8-foot for a 4- or 5-weight line. He built these rods using milling machines and planing forms of his own design. Both of Jenkins's sons helped produce the rods.

"At that point I was mainly involved with winding rods," Steven said.

Production of Jenkins rods peaked in 1975 with fifty rods. By 1986 Charlie was producing very few rods, but Steven was becoming more interested in the rod-building business.

"Actually what spurred me to get into it was that Dad wasn't really building many rods anymore and I kept hearing people say what wonderful rods they were. I sat back and thought this is something special and I don't want to see it go away, so I got involved," Steven said.

He spent his first five years "learning rod building from the ground up" under the watchful eye of his father.

"I'm still in a way serving an apprenticeship. I probably had the best teacher in the world in terms of what I was trying to do. I learned that you don't make a lot of money building rods, but what you do get is the appreciation of the people who use your rods," Steven said.

Charlie and Steven are a unique rod-building team. Both are involved in the building of every Jenkins rod.

"We both have a milling machine in our house. Dad usually starts off preparing the cane and comes up with the butt section. He then brings it to me, and I make the tips, ferrule it, and finish it. People often call me and ask if my dad is still building rods, like we are two separate entities. I think it's important for people to know that Dad's still building rods and I'm still building rods, but they are the same rods we're building together," Steven said.

The Jenkinses start the rod-building process with well-seasoned Tonkin cane, some of which is pre-embargo cane, meaning it comes from before the Communist takeover in China. All cane is oven tempered. It's flamed if a gutsier, stiffer action is required. The cane is milled into strips and then hand planed to the strict tolerances that are the Jenkins family trademark.

"Everyone who builds rods holds themselves to different degrees of accuracy. It's ego, or pride, or something, but you do it. It's very important. You have to hold a strip to two thousandths of an inch, really, because one strip is only half the diameter of the rod. When you glue all the strips together, you could end up four thousandths off. And let's face it, there's only six thousandths of an inch difference between a rod for a 4-weight line and a rod for a 5-weight line," Charlie said.

Once the strips are glued together to form blanks, Steven finishes them with a polyurethane varnish. Unlike some rod builders, he varnishes the blank before he wraps the guides. After the blank is varnished, the guides are wrapped and the threads varnished as a separate operation.

The most elusive description of any fine fly rod is its action. If I had to pick a word to describe the action of the Jenkins rod, I'd say fluid as it's among the most fluid fly rods I have ever cast. There are no hitches in the rod's action. You can smoothly cast just the leader and then move effortlessly to middle casting distances. At the long end the rod continues to load and cast well until its design limits are reached. The line literally glides through the guides. When I cast a Jenkins rod, I get a feeling of effortless casting reminiscent of some Garrison tapers. The rods are also incredibly accurate. You look at where you want the fly to go, and it goes there. The world is a good place when you are casting a Jenkins rod.

"The terms used to describe a rod's action mean different things to different people, but I would describe the action that we've been most successful with as what they used to call just a plain medium dry fly action. There's nothing extreme about it. It isn't a swelled butt. It isn't a big tip with a parabolic action where everything happens in the butt. It's not light where all the action is in the tip. It's a fairly smooth progression—kind of old-fashioned, I guess," Charlie said.

I am drawn to the looks of a Jenkins rod, too. It's very clean, almost spartan. You won't see any of the "jewelry" or bells and whistles that adorn other cane rods. Both Steven and Charlie explain their fly rod's classic good looks by calling it, and themselves, low-key.

The four rods in their standard series typically include a reel seat made with modified Strubble cap and slip ring hardware. The insert, or arbor, is mortised cherry or walnut. The cork handle is bullet shaped. Guides are hard chrome wrapped with honey yellow thread. There is no tipping. Rod sections are joined with Swiss-type ferrules wrapped brown.

The Jenkinses honor customer requests for custom or special cosmetic materials when building one of their standard models to order, but I like Charlie's attitude.

"We'll do anything on the standard model; you know tiger wood and all that stuff may be great for the insert, but cherry is a good old American wood and we think it's beautiful and walnut's pretty nice, too. We like using those woods," he said.

Just recently the Jenkinses have come out with a new line of rods they call the Original C. W. Jenkins Fly Rod. The rod is produced in the same lengths and line weight models as the Jenkins standard line, but the Original will be built as close to the specifications of Charlie Jenkins's original rod as possible. The Original will be sold as offered with no modifications. It's a gorgeous cane rod.

The reel seat hardware is a nickel silver formed cap with tapered ring mounted on a cherry wood arbor that is not mortised. The bullet-shaped cork grip is 6 inches long. The cane is oven tempered and equipped with oxidized Swiss-type ferrules and black chrome guides. The signature and ferrule wraps are brown tipped with yellow and wine. Guide wraps are brown tipped with yellow. A distinctive raised and fixed-ring hook keeper, the same as seen on the original Jenkins rod, is included.

The Original C. W. Jenkins Fly Rod will come in a brass tube and include a ferrule plug of brass and wood matching the arbor. It is classic Jenkins work—meticulous, accurate, clean, and beautiful. It will also be the kind of rod that you won't have the heart to hide away in a collection or hang over the fireplace. It will be the kind of rod you fish. Charlie and Steven wouldn't have it any other way.

It will also be the kind of rod that you would gladly stand out in a frozen school yard at five degrees below zero just for the chance to cast.

April 2001. There was a time when I just about lived on the South Platte River in Cheeseman Canyon. I was new to fly fishing then, Cheeseman Canyon was close to home, and I thought there was no better trout fishing to be had in the state of Colorado. The rainbows (or sometimes cutbows) were huge, and the brown trout made dry fly fishing one of the most challenging pleasures I'd ever known.

Over the years I stopped going into the canyon with the kind of fanatical regularity I did twenty-five years ago. I could say that the crowds have turned me away, but fly fishers have always made their way to Cheeseman Canyon. If seeing other anglers means a place is crowded, then I'd have to say it was crowded twenty-five years ago. I can't even put the blame on whirling disease, which has severely impacted the river a few miles downstream at Deckers. The fact is that I've seen the trout populations go up and down in the canyon before the arrival of whirling disease and they are better now than they were in some of those years.

I can say, and I hope you understand that it is honestly without braggadocio, that in my time I fished the canyon right up there with the best of them. In my case it just worked down to time on the water. I literally fished from eight in the morning until dark four or five days a week. Some of my best memories of those years are walking out of the canyon after dark and listening to the owls hooting back and forth to each other across the river.

As good as I may have been then, I can say that I am now little more than an amateur fly fisher in the canyon. There are some young guns fishing it nowadays with amazing proficiency. I understand how they do it, too, because they are the young men and women who have it so bad that they are fishing the dawn to dark shift that I fished when I was their age.

I was in the canyon last week under what I considered extraordinary circumstances. John Gierach had loaned me his vintage two-piece 8-foot C. W. Jenkins bamboo fly rod. This particular rod was made by Charlie Jenkins at the zenith of his career in the 1960s. John had wrapped a note around the rod that said, "Here's the Charlie rod. Keep it as long as you need it. I like the simple, plain good looks of it."

I think the idea was that I would cast the rod a bit on the lawn with the recommended 5-weight double-taper fly line, report that it was a solid medium dry fly action, and take it back over to John when I was through. But I ended up in Cheeseman Canyon fishing my pal's irreplaceable vintage bamboo fly rod because I couldn't not do it. Charlie Jenkins himself had told me that this very rod evolved around a group of serious fly fishermen who spent a lot of their time in Cheeseman Canyon. What could I do?

I assembled the rod at the picnic table near what is now called the Family Pool. The 6-inch grip is bullet shaped. The distinctive cherry reel seat is flattened to accept the reel foot with a nickel silver cap and tapered ring. "C. W. Jenkins" is engraved on the end of the cap. The Swiss-style ferrules are oxidized and wrapped in brown tipped with yellow and wine. The signature winding has the same wrap and tipping. The line guides and tip-top are chrome and wrapped brown tipped yellow. A serial number appears on a flat above the signature wrap and above the ferrule on both tips. The cane is oven tempered. It's a medium honey color. The three-and-three node work is compact and clean. The overall effect of the cosmetics is as clean, simple, and elegant as I have ever seen. The rod is sweet. And it is legendary on this water.

I cast tiny dry flies over the very difficult trout that work the Family Pool's glassy water. I never got a strike, but I did get a few very close looks, which can almost be considered success on that very tough water. The rod casts like a dream on the required close-in casts and has enough reserve power to gracefully reach the bank risers 50 feet away on the other side of the river. I am a devotee of the medium-action dry fly rod because it makes me a better caster. This rod is among the most pure examples of that action I have come across. Tight loops without a hint of shock waves are easy to cast. Something pleasant happens when casting the rod at moderate to longer distances. I'd describe it as a "power surge." If you hold back just a bit and let the rod do its job, it's amazingly smooth and comfortable to cast.

Eventually I worked my way upstream. There was a smattering of the somewhat larger, darker blue-winged olives that we used to call blue quills, and the trout were on the fin. I spotted several fish holding in a familiar run. I could see the bright red stripes on the sides of the rainbows and the darker, more stream-lined shapes of a few sleek brown trout. And then I spotted a gargantuan rainbow trout. The fish was up close to a gravel bar on the other side of the channel. It was one of those phantom monster trout that show up once in awhile in Cheeseman Canyon. These are trout that keep the young guns on the river from dawn to dark.

I don't have nerves of steel anymore when it comes to very large trout. They rattle me to my core. I didn't have a plan when I started casting at this one. I just started throwing my stuff at him. He finned calmly in the current for the duration of my barrage of casts. Occasionally he moved an inch or two to safely avoid the fly or leader. Eventually, he went off the feed.

I sat down on the bank to collect myself. It occurred to me that if I could conjure up the old magic I could catch this trout. I looked out at the lie and remembered fishing it hundreds of times. And then I remembered the trick. If you stood by a certain rock in a certain way to make the cast, you'd get a perfect drift. I hadn't thought about it for years.

The trout was feeding again when I sneaked back to the river. I stood by the rock just right and made the cast. The trout drifted neatly up under the fly and took it without hesitation. He smoked 35 feet of fly line off the reel before I could think. The trout then bolted downstream into an obstacle course of rocks. I held the rod high. I maneuvered the fly line over one rock. I slipped and almost fell in the river. The fish was still on. He wrapped me on another smaller rock. I finessed the leader off. The trout made a run. I thought that I'd held the fish, but suddenly the electricity went out of the line. It was over.

My sweetheart, who had been painting watercolors on the opposite bank of the river, had seen everything.

"At least you didn't break the rod!" she called out.

It occurred to me that I hadn't even considered John's fly rod. A shudder of fear ran through me. I thought that maybe if I had broken the rod I could have talked Charlie Jenkins or his son Steven, who has taken over much of the Jenkins rod-making business, into fixing the rod for me. They would surely have understood.

Then I remembered. John has fished Cheeseman Canyon as long as I have. He would know that I wasn't fooling about hooking one of the phantoms. He would understand that the Jenkins rod was made to fish.

May 2001. Steven Jenkins agrees that his father, Charlie, and he make fly rods to be fished. "Let's face it, you can have something that looks beautiful, but if it's a fishing rod and it isn't functional, what do you have? I guess you could hang it on the wall," he said.

Steven said that he still works together with his father to produce the same kind of rod that Charlie envisioned for Cheeseman Canyon fly fishers in the 1960s.

"We really haven't gotten on the bandwagon about changing anything on these rods. We're pretty happy with what we're putting out," he said.

Steven said that they did change the names of the rod models, but the tapers are the same. The C. W. Jenkins Original is now called the C. W. Jenkins Classic. The Standard is now the Signature. Signature rods are available in two-piece or three-piece models. The Classic, like Charlie Jenkins's original Cheeseman Canyon model, is available only in two pieces.

"There's no difference in the action between the Signature and the Classic other than the cosmetics. We do make a flame-tempered Signature model that some people say is a little faster than the oven-tempered model, but I think it takes someone who has cast a lot of rods to notice it. It's a subtle difference," Steven said.

Jenkins said that although his father lives in Denver, Colorado, and he is now living in Glenwood Springs, Colorado, they have a system worked out where his dad starts the rods and gets the butt sections glued up and then sends the butt along with the strips for the tips to Steven in Glenwood Springs to be finished.

It's a great collaboration that results in a sweet casting fly rod. I like the idea that a rod was designed for one of my favorite places to fish and that that rod has stood the test of time. It's a rod that compels you to take it fishing—and that is the very best kind of fly rod.

CHAPTER EIGHT

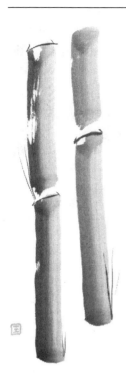

Glenn Brackett and the R. L. Winston Rod Company

December 1999. Fly fishers recognize the name Winston. Some words are just synonymous with the sport. Winston fly rods are the rods with history—the rods that have been around forever. When it comes to bamboo, they are the hollow-fluted, light-weight rods that were the darlings of National Casting Tournament record holders such as Marvin Hedge, G. L. McLeod, and Dick Miller. They are also the rods with the fabulous duronz ferrules and the signature golden amber line guide wraps. These are the rods that are easy on the eyes when you look at them. And casting a Winston is heaven.

Lew Stoner and Robert Winther bought the Western Fishing Rod Company in San Francisco just after the stock market crash in 1929. That's when they combined the letters from both their last names to come up with the name Winston Rod Company and began making superlative bamboo fly rods. Winther sold his

Glenn Brackett

interest in the company to Walter "Red" Loskot in 1933. Loskot was an avid angler and member of the Golden Gate Angling and Casting Club.

In 1934 Stoner's interest in tournament casting, along with Loskot's encouragement, led him to develop the hollow-fluted rod, where the inside apex of the triangular strips used to build a cane rod were removed, resulting in a hollow interior. The result was a lightweight, extremely powerful rod that tournament casters used to break numerous world distance-casting records.

When Doug Merrick came into the shop in 1945 to buy a rod, he ended up staying on as an employee and eventually bought Loskot's interest in the company. Merrick was a natural at rod making and learned much from Stoner, who died suddenly in 1957. Merrick introduced changes in the rod tapers that made them more suitable for anglers, as opposed to Stoner's tapers, which were designed more toward the needs of tournament distance casters. Gary Howells joined the company in 1957 and under the tutelage of Merrick became one of the premier rodmakers in America. Howells left the company in 1969 to form his own storied rod-making operation.

Merrick sold his interest in Winston to Tom Morgan in 1973. Morgan then brought Glenn Brackett into the operation in 1974. Brackett grew up in a fishing family and spent his youth fiddling with old rods—refinishing them and redesigning them. His father worked within a stone's throw of the Winston rod shop, where Brackett hung out as a kid. He also frequented the Golden Gate Angling and Casting Club. Brackett eventually became a fishery biologist with the California Fish and Game Department and the U.S. Fish and Wildlife Service. He continued to fish and tie flies commercially for the fifteen years he spent as a biologist.

Brackett helped Morgan move the company to Twin Bridges, Montana, in 1975 because the fishing was better there, a logical continuation of a tradition at Winston where the rodmakers were all avid fishermen themselves. Howells, Morgan, Merrick, and Al Talbott all contributed to Brackett's development as a rodmaker. He became a part owner of the company in 1976. In 1991 David Ondaatje bought the company from Morgan and Brackett. Brackett stayed on as the manager of the bamboo shop. Morgan still works closely with the company as president emeritus and consultant.

So it all boils down to me anxiously standing by the window with all this history swirling around in my head. I'm waiting for the UPS truck to rumble up my street. It's late November and the first snowstorm of the season is predicted, but it's sunny and warm today. Glenn Brackett has agreed to send me a Winston bamboo fly rod to try out. It's one that he personally recommends.

I hear the truck before I see it. When it stops in front of my house, I race out to the driver.

"Anything for me?" I gasp. There is a pleading look in my eyes. He hands me a long triangular cardboard box that I have come to know will contain a fly rod.

"Oh, thank you, thank you, thank you," I say. When I'm safely inside, I hack open the top and pull out a dark brown aluminum tube with a brass-colored cap and collar. Below the collar is a black label that says, "R. L. Winston Rod Co., Fine Rods Since 1929, Twin Bridges, Montana."

Inside the tube is a three-piece 7-foot 9-inch bamboo rod for a 4- or 5-weight line. It has down-locking nickel silver hardware on the reel seat. The pocketed butt cap has a knurled disk on the end. In the center it says, "R. L. Winston Rod Co." The heavier-than-usual sliding ring is knurled on both ends. The threaded screw lock ring is diamond knurled. I don't know my woods, but I can say that the color of the mortised spacer wood nicely matches the golden amber of the line guide wraps. The cigar grip is pleasingly plump for my long large hand. Then there is the winding check. It's bamboo and it is gorgeous. A ring-style hook keeper is wound with the golden amber thread tipped in burgundy.

The signature wrap begins just above the hook keeper and consists of five wraps—two burgundy standing trim wraps, a wider golden amber wrap, and two more burgundy standing trim wraps. It's followed by "R. L. Winston" on one flat. On the flat directly below that, the rod length, number of sections and tips designation, recommended line weight, and serial number appear. Several inches farther up the rod, a burgundy standing trim wrap, a golden amber wrap, and another burgundy standing trim wrap complete the signature wrap.

The agate in the stripping guide is stunning. It's mostly a clear, very pale tan with four clouds of amber color floating through it. The guide is wrapped in golden amber with no tipping. The renowned duronz ferrule is wrapped for its entire length in golden amber thread and tipped burgundy, which is a signature feature on Winston rods. Ferrules on the midsection and tips are similarly wrapped. Snake guides are wrapped in untipped golden amber. The serial number appears just above the male ferrule on the mid-section. The serial number and tip number (1 or 2) appear above the male ferrule on the tip sections. The tip-tops are wrapped in golden amber and tipped burgundy.

The dark honey color of the cane is immaculately varnished. Node work is compact and fine and staggered in a standard three-and-three stacked node pattern, where a node alternates with a clear nodeless strip and then another node and so on.

Without further ado I grab a reel with a 4-weight double-taper line and one with a 5-weight double taper and head out to cast the rod. I forego my normal casting area in the town park because it's a warm Saturday before a snowstorm. The park is crowded. I head to a more private grassy field that I know of just west of town. I want this to be a private date.

When assembling the rod, I can't resist pulling the ferrules apart and putting them back together a few times. I have come to know similar ferrules on a couple of Gary Howell's rods that I own. Assembling and disassembling the rod is so satisfying that it verges on the sensuous. They are perfectly fitted, and the duronz material has a self-lubricating quality. There is a subdued "pop" when the ferrules are gently disassembled, and they literally glide together when assembled to create a firm, full, and solid fit. I think they are among the best ferrules in the world.

I mount the reel with the 5-weight double-taper line first. The rod casts well close-in, but it is in its glory at real angling ranges of 15 to 45 feet. The big surprise is when I crank out more line and single haul and then double haul the cast. The rod's a lion at long distance. Even allowing for my primitive casting skills, I easily shoot line out to 80 feet and would have gone longer if the kinks in the seldom used 85- to 90-foot section of my fly line had been straightened before the cast. I simply did not expect so much line to come into play.

It is rare to have this kind of controlled power in a 7-foot 9-inch rod. It's responsive throughout the range of casting distances. The rod is lively, light, and sensitive, but still ready to romp at distance. In addition, the rod is capable of picking up a surprising length of line. It casts tight loops on demand with few or no shock waves.

Toward the end of my session with the 5-weight double taper, a bit of a head wind came up. The rod was perfectly at home casting straight into the wind. It cut the crosswind beautifully with very little drift.

The casting characteristics with the 4-weight double taper were amazingly similar to the 5-weight. It was only slightly less responsive when cast very close-in. I may have lost 5 feet when casting for distance. Either weight line casts beautifully, which leaves room for the personal tastes of a wide range of casters.

Glenn Brackett was in the bamboo shop when I called a few days later. After gushing over the rod for several minutes, I mentioned that I hadn't seen the 7-foot 9-inch length rod listed in the Winston catalog.

"We make a lot of rods that we don't list in the catalog. Basically, we make rods in 3-inch increments through a variety of lengths upon request from customers or, actually, in any reasonable increment they want. We'll make rods in metric increments for our Japanese customers," Brackett said.

Brackett said that he has found that most anglers have their own peculiarities when it comes to rod lengths.

"I'm not really keen on 8-foot rods and I think a 7½-foot rod is kind of short. So I cut the difference in half and ended up with the 7-foot 9-inch rod."

I then asked him about the Winston ferrule and fluted hollowing that are the signature of the Winston cane rods.

"We make the ferrules here from solid stock, as opposed to tubular stock, which throws some interesting twists into the picture if you make your own ferrules. The duronz has some aluminum in it which makes it 30 percent lighter than nickel silver. There are some real tricks to working with it that I learned from Gary [Howells] and also through my own work," he said.

Brackett mentioned that although Howells left Winston before the move to Montana he spent many summers fishing in Montana. When in Montana he'd stop by the shop to tutor and encourage both Brackett and Jeff Walker, the other full-time rod builder in the Winston bamboo shop.

The fluted hollowing in rod sizes where it's used typically results in a rod that is semihollow for three-quarters of its length. The bamboo is left solid around the ferrules for added strength. The fluted hollowing, which Lew Stoner developed to reduce the weight in tournament casting rods, is especially noticeable in rods built for the heavier line weights. At one point Stoner developed a 10-foot rod that stayed under the $5\frac{3}{4}$-ounce weight limitation required for tournament casting rods. It's a superlative construction technique for salmon and steelhead fly rods.

A unique aspect of the Winston Rod Company is that it is one of very few true production bamboo rod-building operations left in the United States.

"We have two part-time workers in the bamboo shop. Jeff Walker is the other full-timer. He's been here fifteen years. We use a milling machine that was invented by Lew Stoner to make the strips. It has gone through about three remakes since then. Jeff and I share the different aspects of rod making, so it's truly a joint effort. Jeff is better at some aspects of it than I am, so that's what he does. I like it that way because I think it turns out a better product," Brackett said.

Brackett said that they build a hundred rods per year. A little better than half of those rods are presold, with the others held as stock for dealers. The serial numbers on those rods are witness to the longevity of the company.

"The serial numbers started in the late 1920s at one thousand. When they reached ten thousand sometime in the late 1950s, we started again at one thousand. We have complete records from five thousand on. We're in the three thousands now," Brackett said.

Brackett said anglers have their choice of uplocking, down-locking, or slide bands for reel seat hardware. Grips are typically half wells or cigar shaped, but there is room for a fly fisher's specific requests. There are unlimited options for the wood spacer in the reel seat, and Brackett often encourages people to send in their own wood, which he will finish and install. Reel seat hardware is manufactured for Winston by REC. The agate stripping guide comes from Daryll Whitehead. The snake guides and tip-top are produced by Pacific Bay.

I did notice that the snakes were a bit larger than I had typically seen on other rods of similar length. It could be that the somewhat larger guides are partially responsible for the extra distance I achieved on my casts with the rod.

The hook keeper is Brackett's own design and manufactured on-site at Twin Bridges. The bamboo winding check has become a signature feature for Winston. It is included on every rod unless an alternative is specifically requested. The wrapped ferrules are also another signature feature, along with the golden amber threads on the guides. All rods are finished with a sprayed varnish.

"It's a sprayed finish, which is a unique aspect of our operation. The rod is completely finished minus its reel seat," Brackett said.

Brackett said that he really hasn't made any changes in the progressive tapers that Doug Merrick came up with during his years at Winston.

"They're pretty much the tapers that were being used when I stepped up to the bench. Doug Merrick did the refining on them, so we just stepped into his shoes. The only variation has been putting out three-piece rods and all those other odd rod models, but they still have that characteristic Winston progressive taper," he said.

Brackett said that he has experimented with a variety of rod configurations while at Winston.

"I make anything that's reasonable. I've even played around with spey rods on the upper extreme and occasionally with one-piecers at very short lengths. We've also looked into ferrules made with synthetic materials for certain applications like saltwater fishing, where you're really trying to lighten the rod or eliminate a dead spot. There's really a lot of new technology available, but most people adhere to the old, traditional ways," he said.

Brackett is also known for his introduction of the four-strip cane rod to the Winston catalog.

"I also make a five-stripper and an eight-stripper, but we don't advertise these. It's just another aspect of the craft. It shows we have that capability. It basically came out of the repair business. I love repair work. I've probably learned more about this business and gained more appreciation for the craft and its history through repairs than anything else. And the simple fact is that if you do repairs, sooner or later you'll be faced with a four-strip or five-strip rod and learn how to build a replacement section. That leads to building a rod," he said.

I asked Brackett why he sent me a 7-foot 9-inch rod when Winston is most renowned for its big rods.

"About 90 percent of the rods we make are around that size. It's rare that we build anything larger than that. We do make a few steelhead rods each year, and we make a Haig-Brown commemorative salmon rod that's been on the market for a number years. The money goes toward salmon restoration and studies," he said.

That's when I let it slip that I have a thing for cane rods built for heavier line weights.

"I love big rods. I certainly use them in my steelhead fishing. They offer a number of benefits. I'm a big believer in bamboo as a building material for big rods," he said.

Brackett said that Winston's big rods are built along the same design ideas as the trout rods but offer a 20 to 25 percent reduction in rod weight.

"The weight reduction is much more noticeable in the big rods. Weight is affected quite a bit by the nickel silver hardware, which is unbelievably heavy, but nobody wants to change it because we're so stuck in tradition. Actually, the weight issue was remedied nicely when Winston introduced Bakelite reel seats a long time ago. It's almost weightless. I'd be using it today if we were in that kind of marketplace, but everything has to do with eye appeal now. There are some wonderful metals out there today that could really complement the lightweight aspects of fluted hollowing, but no one wants to take that innovative step," he said.

Brackett said that he hears time and again how anglers come away from a day's fishing with a big cane rod feeling better than if they had used an equivalent graphite rod.

"I think they are a far better fishing tool. You don't have to beat yourself up all day trying to make the rod bend. They are also much better for roll casting and spey casting than graphite, except in very long lengths. Doug Merrick used to say that the test of a well-designed rod is how it roll casts. If it does it well, you've got yourself a good rod. Bamboo is just a great material if you design around it properly. It has that reserve power that graphite never has. It loads smoothly over a continuum," he said.

Brackett said that the real argument shouldn't be over how much a rod weighs, but rather over its action.

"People are starting to think for themselves because they have built up some fishing experience. Seventy-five percent of the people who order bamboo rods from me are ready for a bamboo rod, and there's no need to talk them into it. They're ready to experience what bamboo has to offer and that's wonderful. Typically those people are ten to fifteen years into their fishing and they know what they want, have thought it through, and have educated themselves. Cost doesn't come into it," he said.

Brackett said that although the cost of a bamboo rod may seem a little overwhelming at first, when you look at it over the course of time it's one of the least expensive investments you'll ever make in the sport. He said that there are too many other accouterments that you'll outlive. A cane rod's value increases over time and can be passed down through a family.

Finally, Brackett said that he's just tickled to see all the new interest in bamboo rods and rod making.

"It's really the hobbyist that is keeping the craft alive. A lot of good people are trying to revive interest in bamboo rods and making their knowledge available to everyone. I really encourage that. There are no secrets in this business. It boils down to the same factor that everyone of us faces. It's just a lot of damn hard work," he said.

As for me, I'm delighted that dedicated rodmakers like Glenn Brackett are still happily making the fly rods I dream about.

CHAPTER NINE

Split-Cane Diary: South Creek Ltd.

December 6, 1993—Sent Mike Clark the down payment.

MIKE CLARK IS THE BAMBOO FLY ROD–BUILDING GURU WHO LIVES in Lyons, Colorado. He can turn Tonkin cane into a fly rod that will bring romance into your life. A week with a Clark rod and you'll be ready to propose marriage. I know that for a fact. A John Gierach–A. K. Best Special Taper 8½-foot split-cane fly rod for a 5-weight line that Mike built has been my constant companion for a number of years. Ordering this new rod verged on bigamy.

The down payment was just the beginning of the process. The waiting came next.

There is a blackboard on the wall in Mike's shop. It lists names. Beside those names are notations like "8½, 2/2 [two-piece, two tips], 5 wt." There are three columns of names and rod descriptions. Your name goes at the bottom of the list when Mike

Mike Clark

PHOTO BY KATHY SHULKIN-JENSEN

receives your order. No exceptions. The list always has fifty or sixty names on it. Mike handcrafts about forty fly rods a year. When you're on the bottom line, it means you wait. Figure about a year and a half.

Nowadays a year-and-a-half wait for anything is unusual. That wasn't always the case. In decades past we were a nation of patient waiters. Pioneers often waited six or seven months just for the mail to arrive.

The rod I ordered was not fancy. Nothing more than a sister to my 5-weight. I liked the 5-weight so much that I wanted a 6-weight in the same taper and length. But the wait is the same.

February 10, 1994—Sent Mike Clark a note. Changed the order to 8-foot, 6-weight, three-piece model. Better for airplanes.

May 12, 1994—Changed rod order again. Went for Clark's Labrador Special, a three-piece 8-foot beauty for a 7-weight forward line. Rod includes a 2-inch detachable fighting butt. Figure it will be a good Montana rod and double as a light bass rod. Maybe some day I'll even get to Labrador. A real change. I don't have any heavy cane rods. I need this. The deeply flamed bamboo and fighting butt are pure sex.

August 19, 1994—It would have never worked out between me and the Labrador Special. Let's face it, when am I ever going to get to Labrador?

August 21, 1994—Called Mike. I've ordered a three-piece 8-foot for a 5-weight. I want a rod that will compel me to fish Colorado's uplands because that is where I live. I've ordered a light tip for fishing the small streams that have their headwaters in the high lakes. The other tip will be heavier for the longer casts necessary when I make it to the lakes.

Throughout the entire process Mike patiently listened to me. Every time I changed the order, he just said, "No problem." I don't think he even wrote the changes down, at least not until this one. He somehow knew this was the one. I asked him if any of his other customers are as indecisive as I am.

"It happens all the time," Mike said.

The changes don't increase the cost of the rod unless additional details such as extra wraps or fancy engraving on the hardware are added. A custom-built split-cane fly rod can cost anywhere from about $900 up. It's important to note that not everyone who fishes bamboo rods is wealthy. I wished it was that easy, because then I wouldn't have to wonder where I was going to come up with the money.

I can't make a case for a bamboo fly rod being better than, equal to, or anything like a graphite rod. That's the point. There are no comparisons. You like cane or you don't. I knew I liked it the first time I saw a well-made, handcrafted split-cane rod. It wasn't the price or even the exquisite workmanship. Split-cane rods are beautiful to look at. And then you cast one. Each rod has personality, subtleness, and a few secrets. A superior split-cane rod is sensuous to cast. Graphite rods are great, but you're not going to take one home to meet the folks.

February 24, 1995—Mike Clark called. My rod is near the top of the list. "This is it. Do you want to change anything?" he asked. I said no. "Okay, you better start thinking about the details—reel seat, handle, the color of the wraps. Let me know."

The details were easier than I thought. I looked through the cork handle designs in the rod section of Ernest Schwiebert's book, *Trout,* and decided on the one that Jim Payne, a venerated cane rod builder, used on his standard trout fly rod. Mike called it a western style. I opted for an uplocking, blued reel seat with a walnut spacer. I chose to have the bamboo deeply flamed because I like the way it looks. It also quickens the action of the rod just a bit.

The line guide wraps were the hardest decision. I called Mike and we talked about it. When I blurted out that I wanted the wraps to be the colors on a cutthroat trout, I knew I'd picked the right fly rod. I finally understood that what I'd wanted all along was a cutthroat trout rod.

Mike suggested olive and burnt orange wraps—the colors on a Greenback cutthroat trout. As an afterthought I said, "Let's inscribe 'The Cutthroat Special' on the rod."

February 26, 1995—Called Mike. Asked him if I could come and watch him make my rod. Said I wouldn't be a nuisance. I just wanted to see it all. He hesitated, then said yes.

You have to know rodmakers. They are a cranky lot, right up there with commercial fly tiers. Something primal goes on when a master rod builder starts eyeing a piece of bamboo. Building a split-cane rod is not a high-tech procedure. The basic tools are a micrometer, a set of forms, and a plane. They have changed little from the first split-cane rods built in the mid-1800s. What makes the rod is the builder's experience, instinct, and perseverance.

A rod builder will never tell you that. He'll just run a stream of taper designs, micrometer readings, and line guide specs past you. He will tell you that it's all engineering.

March 5, 1995—At Mike's shop. He showed me the cane that will become the Cutthroat Special. Half a culm of bamboo has already been split in appropriate pieces and flamed. It's tied in a neat bundle at the foot of the workbench.

The bamboo culms (culm means jointed stem of grass) come in bundles of twenty. Each culm is 12 feet long. Most of Mike's have come from Charles Demarest, Inc., in Bloomingdale, New Jersey. The bamboo must be aged. Mike uses cane seven to fifteen years old.

The bamboo used to make fly rods is *Arundaria amabilis*. That translates to "the beautiful reed." Most aficionados simply know it as Tonkin cane. It is grown in the Sui River drainage in the Guangdong Province of southern China, a region notorious for its fierce monsoon winds. Rod builders and rod users alike believe that the bamboo's evolution to resist these winds has resulted in the strong fibers that account for the superior casting qualities of rods made from Tonkin cane.

The great art and mystery in the rod builder's trade is his ability to select the single culm of bamboo that can be made into the particular fly rod he has in mind. Most builders can't tell you exactly how they do it.

The Tonkin cane grows to a height of about 40 feet. The 12-foot section that Mike uses to build a rod comes from toward the bottom to the middle of that 40 feet. The three sections of my rod will come from a continuous section of bamboo fiber. "The fiber needs to be continuous because then we can take advantage of nature's engineering," Mike said. The best split-cane rod is more the result of an appreciation of the bamboo's innate nature than a feat of engineering. Master rod builders try to capture the monsoon winds in their fly rods.

"Each rod I make has its own personality because each piece of cane is different. I can build two identical rods from a specifications point of view, but they will be different because each culm of bamboo is different. The closest I can come to building identical rods would be if I built two from the same culm," Mike told me.

March 6, 1995—Set forms and began planing the rod today.

Ernest Schwiebert quotes the legendary rod builder Jim Payne as saying there are "145 separate operations" that take place when a split-cane rod is built. The most important step is the planing of the bamboo into the triangular-shaped sections that the rodmaker will glue together to form the six-sided rod blank.

The long metal planing form has a V in the middle that forms an angle of sixty degrees. This angle allows each of the six triangular splines to be planed within thousandths of an inch, ensuring that they will fit together perfectly when the planing is complete.

The size of the V can be adjusted along its length to minutely vary the width of the spline that is being planed. These graduated variations are what create the rod taper. All rod builders are interested in tapers, which are the basis of what makes a rod cast the way it does. Beginning rod builders tend to experiment wildly with them. Then, as their skills develop, they find a certain taper or set of tapers that come to define their work.

Mike's John Gierach–A. K. Best Special Taper is one of those defining tapers. It has a crisp, quick dry fly action, especially suited to Rocky Mountain waters.

Rod builders are also interested in the bamboo's nodes. The node is the joint you see when looking at a culm of bamboo, and it's the weakest part of the material. Mike carefully examines the nodes and files them down during the initial phase of the planing operation. When the six splines that form the blank are glued together, Mike will be sure that no nodes are placed adjacent to each other.

Mike begins the planing process by scraping off the excess pith from the inside of the bamboo and removing the inner nodal wall. The inside, pithy part of the bamboo is planed to form two sides of the triangular spline. The enameled outside part of the bamboo, where the power fibers are most numerous, is never planed. Mike does his initial rough planing in a wooden jig and then finishes the job in a metal form, where he brings the spline into the exact specifications required for the six sections to match perfectly when glued together.

"The scariest part is the planing. Nothing ever happens on the first spline. It's always toward the end. If something goes wrong, it's all over because you can't mismatch the pieces. You have to start all over and plane all new pieces from a new culm of bamboo," Mike said.

Mike insists on hand splitting and hand planing his fly rods. Some builders use a machine to mill the tapers. The relative merits of the two techniques are controversial. Purists argue that the fibers will be continuous in a hand-split rod, whereas a milled rod may be cut across the grain of the bamboo, which could weaken the fibers.

The planing process on my rod, the Cutthroat Special, was more complicated than most because I wanted different tapers on the two tips. The planing forms had to be set for the butt section of the rod, the midsection, and twice for the different tips.

"We started with a Ford," Mike grumbled, referring to the rod I first ordered. "And now we're at a Jaguar."

The planing process appeared amazingly simple. Mike simply held the spline in the form and planed the excess off the top of the bamboo until it was perfectly level with the top of the form. He planed the bamboo in smooth, effortless strokes. But I got the feeling it's not as easy as it looks.

March 7, 1995—Planing complete, blanks glued.

When the planing was completed, the pace of the work changed. Mike covered the floor with a piece of cardboard and pulled out a big ball of string and a pot of glue. He put on a work apron.

"I hate this part. I'll be covered in glue all day," he said.

The six splines for each of the four sections of the rod (two tips) are glued together quickly and then bound in spirals of cotton string. The glued and bound sections are placed in a cabinet to dry for two days.

The building of a single rod doesn't consume entire days, except when the splines are planed and glued. Other steps may take a few minutes or a few hours, with periods of inactivity between the drying of the glues, varnish, and color preservers.

"I always have three or four rods going at a time, so that I keep busy," Mike said.

March 8, 1995—The glue on my rod is drying. Mike works on other rods.

The break is a good time to talk about the details of the rod. Standard Super Swiss ferrules are the best. The stainless steel Standards are similar to the legendary Super-Z's. Mike uses reel seats from Research Engineering Corporation—"They're the best there is." Snake line guides are stainless steel and come from Pacific Bay.

Mike will use an agate stripping guide on my rod. "No one makes agate line guides any more," he said. "They're all antiques. Daryll Whitehead is a major source. He found a bunch of them a few years ago."

Most of the cork for rod handles comes from Spain and Portugal. "I get the best I can, but the high-quality cork goes to the wine and champagne industry. We get what's left over. In a bad cork year it isn't great," Mike said.

Mike is noticeably more relaxed after the planing is complete. The detail work, such as attaching the ferrules, reel seat, and cork handle and wrapping the line guides, is important, but errors or glitches can often be corrected.

March 9, 1995—Mike removes the strings, scrapes off the excess glue, lightly sands and polishes the blank. He straightens the rod tips a little over a flame. In the afternoon he glues the ferrules, cork handle, tip-top line guide, and reel seat on the blank.

Everything on a Clark rod is open to negotiation. Mike wants you to decide on the color of the line guide wraps, shape and size of the cork handle, and whether the hardware should be blued. My hand is big, long, and thin. I've never bought a fly rod off the shelf that fit it. Mike builds and shapes a handle on the spot to fit me. It's longer (6½ inches) and fatter than most. It feels just right.

March 12, 1995—Returned to Mike's. In my absence he has wrapped the guides. The rod is beautiful. I assembled it and wiggled it around a bit. The action is sublime. It's a hair on the slow side. I like that. If I could have described the action best suited for what the rod must do, this would be it. The point is I couldn't describe this action. I don't know how Mike does it.

I have to leave tonight. I won't be around when Mike puts three or four coats of varnish over the wraps and then painstakingly dips the rod in spar varnish. He will then place it

in a dust-free drying cabinet for two or three days. After that he'll
polish it and put it back into the drying cabinet, because the pol-
ish tends to soften the varnish.

When he takes it out of the cabinet, he'll remove the residue
of the polish and the rod will be done.

April 2, 1995—Mike called. A series of wind storms in Lyons has
set him back. He doesn't want to varnish the rod with all the dust
flying around in the air.

April 7, 1995—Mike called. The rod is done. The problem is I can't
go get it until I get back from a business trip to L.A.

April 20, 1995—Met Mike on the South Platte River for the blue-
winged olives. He brought the rod.

It was in a black tube. I eased the rod bag from the case. The
rod smelled of varnish. It was gorgeous. One flat, just above the
wraps at the top of the handle, had "South Creek Ltd., mc"—
Mike's company and his initials. Another flat had "Michael D.
Clark maker." Still another was inscribed with "#954, 8', 5w."

Finally, farther up the same flat was "The Cutthroat Special."

I slid the rod back into the cloth bag. As anxious as I was to
fish it, I didn't want to fish it on the South Platte. I know a little
upland stream with pure-strain native Colorado River cutthroat
trout. I'd waited this long. I'd wait for that stream to open.

CHAPTER TEN

Ted Knott Split-Bamboo Fly Rods

February 1999. Several years ago Canadian rod builder Ted Knott heard that John Gierach was going to be fishing in British Columbia with his long-time friend and fly-fishing guide, Dave Brown. Knott told Brown that if he was guiding Gierach he wanted him "in that boat with a bamboo rod." A few weeks later an 8-foot three-piece split-cane fly rod for a 6-weight line arrived in Brown's mailbox.

"I just thought it was the right thing to do. The rod was a custom job that I built for Dave. I don't get a lot of requests for it, but it was good for the water where they'd be fishing," Knott said.

In a roundabout way the rod Knott sent Brown was part of the reason I was standing down at the local park on a warm February morning test casting a Ted Knott 8-foot three-piece rod for a 5-weight line. As it turns out, Ted didn't stop when he built the rod for Dave. The next year, when John arrived in British

Ted Knott

_{PHOTO BY JOHN RENNISON}

Columbia, this 5-weight rod was waiting for him. I'd been rummaging around in John's rather sumptuous rod rack when I came across it and asked him what the story was. As usual, John just stuck the rod tube in my hand and said, "Give it a try."

It became clear within a few backcasts that Jim Payne's influence was lurking in the rod. I could feel it bending smoothly just above the grip as I false cast line out. Eventually, the action crept subtlety into the grip. That indescribable feeling of subtle symmetry in a rod when cast is as much Jim Payne's signature as anything.

I had fiddled around with line weights on the 8-footer a bit before I got started. It was designated as a 5- or 6-weight, so I'd tried both weights and settled on a Cortland 444 double-taper 5-weight. The rod, matched with that line, wanted to romp. I easily cast it out to 75 feet with a single double haul, and I'm sure it would have been up for more, especially in the hands of a better caster than myself. After the obligatory blast for distance, I concentrated on middle- and close-range casting. Middle-range work was effortless. The fly went obediently to where I pointed the rod. I know that much of this has to do with the caster, but I am convinced that good rod design makes accurate casting easier.

At short ranges the rod had none of the "tippiness" that you sometimes come across in dry fly tapers. That was pleasing to me because I don't especially like a tippy rod, particularly if it's to be used in the West, but some casters may initially find the somewhat stouter tip a bit of a distraction. I didn't, and happily made delicate casts with little more than 3 or 4 feet of fly line extending from the tip-top guide.

"I have noticed that some rods that are designed to cast in close are pretty wimpy in the tip, so one of the things I do when I'm tweaking a taper is to beef the tip up a little. I use my casting to make the rod do the short stuff, rather than the tip of the rod," Knott said.

The slightly heavier tip was in line with Knott's overall plan for the rod, which he described as "something a little beefier for western fishing that at the same time could handle a 5-weight line."

Knott came to building split-cane rods by a little different route than other builders.

"The first time I thought about building a bamboo rod was back in the 1950s. I was working as a tool and die designer for International Harvester at the time. A few of us were keen fishermen, and we got hold of a George Herter book on rod building. I looked at it, but never did anything about it because at the time I couldn't get ahold of a planing form. Several years later, when I'd gotten into teaching, I decided to take another crack at it. It took about a year to accumulate the tools," Knott said.

Knott said that he followed the same learning curve as many amateur rod builders. He made one rod the first year, then two or three rods the next year, and then he started making an extra rod to "give away." Before long people were asking him to build rods for them and offering him money.

"It went on like that until I retired. I decided then to begin making rods to order for people. I probably made my first rod twenty-five years ago. I build fifteen or sixteen rods a year now, but I also spend time on repair work and restorations," Knott said.

Knott said that his rods have continued to evolve, even from the one John loaned me to test cast.

"That rod had three-by-three node staggering. I've experimented with other kinds of node staggering too, but I now think I've pretty much settled on two-by-two staggering. I just like the looks of it," he said.

Knott said that he has developed several standard rod models that incorporate the influence other rod builders have had on him over the past twenty-five years.

"Over the years every time a rod of any significance came into my hands I measured it and graphed it. I got a real pile of information that way, and after awhile you begin to see patterns emerging that you like," he said.

Knott said that he has been most influenced by the Payne rods, especially in shorter lengths.

"Payne rods typically have a subtle swelling that goes on in the butt. You can't always see it, but if you measure it or graph it out, it's there. It may be one of the things that make the rods special," he said.

In larger rods Knott likes Paul Young's ideas.

"I like Young's big parabolics. They are heavier, powerful rods. Another rod I like in larger sizes is the Hardy CC de France. It's really the only Hardy I like, but it just has this nice relaxed power and it's a pleasure to fish it. If you graph it out, the curve is surprisingly similar to the Garrison rods," Knott said.

With these influences in mind, Knott has come up with four standard rod models: a two-piece 6½-foot, 3-weight rod whose design was influenced by a taper from Wayne Cattanach that Knott changed a little to include a somewhat stiffer tip; a two-piece (also available in three pieces) 7-foot, 4-weight that came out of "a Payne taper with just a little bit of tweaking"; a two-piece 7-foot 6-inch, 5-weight with strong influences from Payne's tapers; and a two-piece 8-foot, 7-weight Light Steelhead rod whose major influence comes from the Hardy CC de France.

"The 7-foot, 4-weight has been adapted a few times so it doesn't quite look like a Payne 98, but you can see the influence. It's a very popular rod and the one I personally like to fish the most," Knott said.

On the shorter length rods Knott uses nickel silver sliding bands on the reel seat. There is a cap on the end. A nickel silver trim ring is secured at the base of the handmade cork grip. The Light Steelhead model utilizes uplocking nickel silver hardware.

"I swag the bands out eight degrees so that when you slide them up on the reel foot the bottom part doesn't dig into the wood. My favorite wood for the insert is tiger-striped maple, unless somebody just absolutely wants something else," Knott said.

Knott flames all his rods to a "tortoiseshell appearance" and stains the tiger-striped maple reel seat insert to "pick up on the flamed color of the rod."

Although Knott's earlier rods included a hook keeper, he stopped using them.

"Invariably, my leader is longer than the rod, so I just bring the leader down around the reel and hook it to the first guide. I figured, why keep it if I don't use it?" he said.

The wraps on standard models are typically brown or burgundy with tipping on the windings on the butt section, on the ferrules, and to designate tip sections. Knott also has a color stick available and will custom wrap the guides to choice. He confesses that his signature wrap does change in color a little once in awhile, but is typically "about $1/4$ to $3/8$ inch of a solid color, plus four turns of the trim color, plus three turns of something in contrast."

A single SIC stripping guide is used on the shorter length standard models, with Pacific Bay snake guides and tip-top guide. The Light Steelhead model has two stripping guides along with larger snake guides and tip-top. The ferrules are Super Swiss–style, manufactured by Classic Sporting Enterprises. Knott prefers the longer standard size ferrule over the truncated version.

At this time Knott hand planes all his rods but isn't opposed to the idea of using a bevelling machine.

"If my volume increased, I'd look pretty hard at a bevelling machine. If you build a lot of rods, it's pretty hard on the wrist, elbows, and shoulders, and anything you can do to get past that first roughing stage is a blessing. Besides, my early training was as a tool and die maker, so I've been kicking around ideas for a machine for as long as I can remember, but they are still on paper," Knott said.

Knott says that in practice he tries to look at each culm of bamboo and then make the best possible use out of its length. The tips on all rods are book matched. Rods are finished with spar varnish that is applied twice to the blank and then wet sanded to maintain the hexagonal shape of the rod. The guides, grip, and other hardware are then mounted. Guide wraps are then finished with polyurethane, which Knott believes best maintains the integrity of the color. The rod is then given a final dip in spar varnish.

Knott partially credits his large file of information on rod designs to his attendance at a number of rod builder gatherings.

"I try a lot of rods because I go to three or four gatherings a year. Once in awhile you come across a rod that you really like," he said.

The fact is that Knott liked the rod-building gathering in Grayling, Michigan, so much that he asked Ron Barch, one of its organizers, if he thought there was room for another one in southern Ontario. Barch encouraged him, and the North Eastern Bamboo Rod Builders Gathering was born three years ago. The gathering takes place near the Grand River, which is a prime brown trout tailwater. The rod builder gathering takes place on Canadian Conservation Authority property where there is a casting pond and a converted barn, which is used for meetings. The "Grand Gathering," as it is known in reference to the Grand River, has been well attended. Typically, two concurrent rod-building sessions are run with one oriented toward beginning cane rod builders and the other directed toward a specialty topic, such as exotic woods, glues, or tapers.

"We hold the gathering on your Memorial Day weekend each year. We've had guys from Nova Scotia, British Columbia, Alberta, Pennsylvania, New York, and Delaware. We also get a pretty good cross section of well-known rod builders that are sort of our heroes up here," he said.

All of it seems to go into the mix when you cast one of Ted's rods. And one of the best parts of it for U.S. citizens is the favorable money exchange between the United States and Canada. Knott's standard models at the time of this writing go for $1,200 Canadian for a two-piece rod and $1,450 Canadian for a three-piece model. Ted said that if you figured the math, it comes out to about $800 U.S. for one of his two-piece rods.

And that is not a bad deal at all for a highly serviceable new split-cane bamboo rod.

October 1999. Mike Clark, the gifted rodmaker from Lyons, Colorado, has left a cryptic message on my telephone answering machine.

"There's a tube here for you from Ted Knott," it said.

I know from past experience that tube can only mean rod tube. And as a rule, rod tubes come with something inside. I call

Mike up and leave a message on his answering machine, saying that I'll make the two-hour drive to Lyons as soon as I can.

A few weeks later I'm standing in Mike's shop holding the silvery aluminum tube in my hands. When I unscrew the cap, I can see the reel seat and tips of a bamboo fly rod. Further inspection indicates that it's a 7-foot two-piece rod. "The Ontario Classic" is written near the butt with the initials "TK." On another strip "7'-0" for #4 DT line, June 20, 1999" is written. There is also a note enclosed in the tube:

> To: Ed Engle
> C/O: John Gierach   Oct. 19, 1999
>
> Ed, I hope that delivery by way of John is OK. I had John's address but not yours.
>
>   Occasionally, one of my rods ends up with minor cosmetic defects. In the case of this one, there are minor glue lines at one of the butt nodes. I will not sell these, but instead give them to friends, conservation draws, etc.
>
>   I can tell from your writing that you clearly enjoy fishing with bamboo. I think that you will like this one. It's my favorite for the Grand River tailwater fishery. I use a #4WF Cortland Clear Creek line most of the time, but occasionally I use a #5WF when fishing up close. The rod evolved from a Payne 98 that I owned for a few years, but which eventually stopped being a Payne and became an airline ticket and several days of guided fishing on the Bow River!!!!!
>
> Regards,
> Ted Knott

The immediate mystery was how a rod sent to John got to Mike Clark's shop, but I quickly figured that out. John had moved and the rod was sent to his old address. It just so happens that the UPS man, who is a fly fisher himself, knew that John shows up at Mike's with clocklike regularity. He rightly assumed that the rod would get to John faster if he left it at Mike's than if he actually tried to deliver it to the new address. Mike knew that a rod delivered to him and addressed to me in care of John would get to me faster if he just called me. This sort of incestuous maneuvering can occur only in backwater endeavors such as the use and collection of split-cane fly rods. It's one of the reasons I like bamboo rods so much.

Upon inspection I find that I'm familiar with the rod if only by reputation. Ted had described it to me as "probably the most popular rod that I make." The taper has its origin in the Payne 98, but Knott "slightly stiffened the tip" to handle the dead-drift nymph fishing on the Grand River, which is his local tailwater. He also mentioned that he slightly reduced the "kick" in the butt section.

The rod features a Payne-style grip, which is also known as a western grip, with the hooded cap for the reel foot concealed under the cork and uplocking nickel silver REC hardware. The insert is stabilized black ash burl. The grip is 6½ inches long. The stripping guide and snake guides are Pacific Bay. Ferrules are standard length from Classic Sporting Enterprises, although Knott also uses REC ferrules. The guides on the butt section are wrapped in brown tipped yellow. The guide wraps on the tip sections are not tipped, but yellow tipping is used at the ferrule and tip-top to designate sections.

The bamboo is flamed to a mottled brown finish. The nodes are staggered two by two. The spar varnish finish is excellent.

I immediately took the rod up to John's house, where we learned what you can learn from casting a rod on the grass. It's a smooth, effortless caster at fishing distances, which I consider to be no more than 40 feet. Casts to 65 feet are easily accomplished with a bit of a single haul. A double haul gets you out even farther, which is pleasing to know, but seldom applies to fishing situations.

Close-in the rod is a little tight, but this is in-line with the slightly "stiffened" tip. Knott's philosophy is that he can use his casting to accomplish what a finer tip can accomplish close-in. That allows him to add a little more to the tip to enhance performance farther out. Changing over from the 4-weight double-taper line to a 5-weight forward line improves performance at close-in ranges.

August 2000. I've hiked into a small stream near Rocky Mountain National Park with the single goal of putting the Ontario Classic through its paces. The water here is mostly pockets, but there's just enough small- to medium-sized pools and slicks to keep your presentations honest. I'm starting at a lower elevation, which means I'm looking at brown trout and brook trout, but I could very well fish my way upstream into cutthroats.

Over the past few years I've changed my mind on small-stream fly rods. At first I thought a tippy, slower rod was the answer. And it is if conditions are fairly civilized, where reasonable backcasts can be made and delicate conditions prevail, but if the country is rough and brushy, I've come to prefer a more stout-tipped rod. A somewhat heavier tip allows me to punch out roll casts in tight quarters, more easily direct and control dapped flies, and make critical short mends through a smaller arc when needed. The Ontario Classic fits the bill here.

Unfortunately, the trout are proving difficult. It's not that I can't catch a few here and there; it's just that it isn't the way it's supposed to be. Small-stream trout are supposed to be playfully easy to catch. A fly, any fly, well presented to water that holds trout should result in a strike. But the majority of these fish are making quick, bright refusal rises or even going as far as bouncing my #14 Yellow Stimulator with their noses like a beach ball.

Switching flies makes no difference, and I know it's not the fly rod. I'm getting the fly exactly where I want it to be. It's a simple case of these small-stream trout not being as dumb as some fishers would have you believe. Still, I pick up the occasional brown trout under an overhanging willow or a bright little brookie at the tail out to a pool. The moral to all of this is to never suppose that any trout, anywhere, anytime, is an idiot.

I'm sitting on the bank after lunch watching the water when I see the first Red Quill spinner hovering over the stream. I know it won't be the only one. It's just a matter of time before I'll see a mating swarm of them. I also know that the Red Quills signal redemption. I have fished this upland country too many years to not know what the Red Quills mean. Every trout that can eat in this little stream will be on the feed.

I switch to an easy-to-see #14 Parachute Red Quill fly pattern for the sake of propriety, but any fly will do. The first cast fools a nice little brown. Every pocket, slick, seam, and tail out that looks like it holds a trout produces a brookie or brown. I fish my way upstream. I am totally absorbed, absolutely in the moment. Everything is perfect.

When I catch the first cutthroat of the day, I pause. It's coppery on the gill plates with large black spots toward the tail and an orange/red slash under the jaw. I take it to be some variation of the Yellowstone cutthroats that were imported here years ago. It's a wonderful trout.

It occurs to me for just an instant that for the last hour or so the Ontario Classic has seemed like an extension of my body. I haven't noticed it at all. To my way of thinking, you can't ask for more in a fly rod.

CHAPTER ELEVEN

George Maurer's Sweetwater Rods

October 1995. The East Gallatin River near Bozeman is the kind of small stream George Maurer would like. It's self-contained, complete within itself. Some anglers would call the brown trout unpretentious, which is another way to say that they are not big. But they suit the water and they are wild.

Several years ago my friend John Gierach handed a George Maurer rod to me when we were fishing the East Gallatin.

"What do you think?" he asked as we exchanged rods and I hefted the Maurer.

I did what I always do when I am handed a cane rod from a maker I'm not familiar with. I cast it short. I've learned over the years that my favorite trout fishing occurs within 30 feet of the rod tip—and that often includes the length of the leader.

This particular rod was an 8-footer for a 5-weight line. The mass of the rod in my hand felt different than most. The weight

George Maurer

seemed to drift toward the tip. It was reminiscent of the unmistakable feel of a Payne.

The rod cast like a dream close-in. I stripped in all the fly line and tried casting just the leader—another one of my quirky rod tests. It was sweet. Finally, I loaded the rod up, double hauled, and shot the fly line upstream. The rod cast distance, too.

I wrote George Maurer when I got back home to Colorado. I told him that I would have to have one of his fly rods. I suggested that we meet.

A few months later I was in front of George's renovated limestone farmhouse near Kutztown, Pennsylvania. There was a stack of Maurer cane rods lying on the hood of my car. I gave each a spin on the broad grassy lawn.

There was a great variety in the actions of the rods I cast that day, but even then I could see that George was beginning to move toward the kind of cane rod that would define his work. He disdained rods that felt like broomsticks when cast. George thought a rod should be fun, even sensuous, to cast. He liked rods that flexed more fully, allowing a somewhat slower action—an action that an angler could feel and appreciate.

You could use the word semiparabolic to describe the action of George's rods, but he'd caution you about it.

"Semiparabolic seems to confuse people and rightly so. There's actually many semiparabolics and they're as different as George Burns and Malcolm X. Garrison's rods are considered semiparabolics, but my rods don't cast anything like his. Throughout cane rod history, the name game has been confusing. Actions are called crisp, medium, dry fly, parabolic, fast, but it all depends on who's describing them," George said.

Maurer suggested that I look at rod design as a straight taper versus a compound taper.

"Straight tapers go evenly from the big end to the small end. A compound taper varies at different places over the total length of the rod to achieve various results in action. I like a light tip with the lever in the middle and then the flex in the butt section. It enables you to have an incredibly tight loop when you want it, but you can open it up, too. That gives you a wider range of control," Maurer said.

The rod that John Gierach handed me on the East Gallatin was the product of George's research into Paul Young's tapers. He applied what he learned about Young's "semiparabolic" rods to traditional tapers. The result was a rod that cast well close-in and also had the power to shoot a lot of line. That rod came to be known in George's catalog as the Trout Bum.

The names of other rod models in George's catalog often reflect their uses. The Wild Creek is a 6½-foot small-stream rod for a 4-weight line. The General is a beefy 8-foot semiparabolic rod for a 6-weight line. Other models are the '48 Special, Spring

Creek, Delaware Special, Bitch Creek, Rocky Mountain Special, and Old Philosopher. The rods are characterized by a flawless varnish finish over flamed, browntone, or golden cane. Hardware is typically nickel silver with Super-Z-style ferrules that can be blued or bright.

Maurer's newest rod is the Rocky Mountain Trout Bum, which is a beefed-up version of the Trout Bum.

"It's designed as a semiparabolic all the way. I didn't mix it up with other tapers. It's semiparabolic straight through. I made it because I figured I might need a more powerful rod with a wider range of big-water applications out West," Maurer said.

He's also been on what he describes as a three-piece rod binge. I like the three-piece rods because they are easier to travel with and the extra ferrule slightly tightens the action. The result is a delightful rod to cast.

"My favorite little creek rod right now is a 7-foot 3-inch three-piece rod that I just finished last spring. It's a 5-weight that I modeled on the taper I used on the two-piece Bitch Creek in my catalog. It's a sweet little rod," George said.

Maurer rounds out his income by offering cane rod-building courses in his shop.

"I offer a hands-on course for two or three people where I guide them through the entire rod-building process. They come out of the course with a finished cane rod and go home with the ability to build their own rods," Maurer said.

In addition to the course, Maurer also has a mail-order business where he supplies cane rod-building components and hard-to-find parts to a growing number of cane rod-building hobbyists.

"I just try to supply the stuff that I had so much trouble finding when I first started building rods," Maurer said.

For several years now it has been my suspicion that although George makes rods in all weights, his heart is in the lighter, smaller rods.

"I make the bigger sticks, but I'll admit that I don't fish them a whole lot. It has a lot to do with where I live here in the East. A lot of our small creeks are difficult to fish, so they're not crowded and they're full of wild trout. That's where I end up fishing a lot," George said.

Maurer's love of small streams and angling/wilderness literature has resulted in two fine small-stream rods named after locations found in the late Harry Middleton's books. The Starlight Creek Special is a fast 7-foot 3-inch, 4-weight for small-stream pocket water. George describes it as a "7-foot Granger speeded up a little." The Starlight Creek is a 7½-foot, 5-weight with a medium-fast "Payne-ish" action.

These and George's other "small" rods are the kind of rods that can transport you to the sort of places that George talks about the most: little creeks where the water is clear and cold, headwaters where you'll never see another angler and all the trout are wild. It's cutthroat and brookie country. It's the sweet water.

July 2000. My sweetheart, Jana, has fallen hard for a '48 Special that George Maurer gave to me in 1994. It's a two-piece 7-footer for a 4-weight line with a blued down sliding ring over a nicely figured dark wood spacer. The wraps are a dark chocolate brown. The stripper looks like a Mildrum. The ferrules are clearly Super-Z style. The bamboo was flamed to a dark honey color. The nodes were staggered in a spiral style. I got the rod because there was a flaw in the butt section that had to be repaired with some invisible wraps.

"It will still fish great," George said at the time.

The '48 Special was my small-stream rod of choice at the time because I admired the smooth Payne-like taper. The rod did everything I asked of it and more on the small Colorado upland streams that I frequented when I wanted to get away from the crowds.

"The '48 Special goes way back. It came about when I'd sorted myself out a bit behind the rod making and began trying to do some tapers of my own rather than just copying, say, a Granger or whatever I got my hands on. I probably went through six or seven models before it evolved into what it is now," George said.

He said that he was using bamboo that he'd gotten from Walton Powell when he came up with the rod. Powell had told him that the bamboo was from 1948, so he named the rod the '48 Special.

"I guess I was using a spiral-style node stagger when I made the rod you have. I was experimenting with several different node staggering styles at the time, but I eventually settled on the Leonard three-and-three style that I now use exclusively," George said.

Maurer said that the '48 Special continues to be one of his more popular rods.

"The only difference now is that I swell the butt on it a little. The taper is kind of a conglomeration. I started with a 7-foot Granger and the Payne 98 and just started merging those ideas and graphing things and then trying again and saying, Let's see what happens if I do this," he said.

The beauty of the '48 Special in Jana's hand is that none of the rod-making details matter to her. She fly-fishes the backcountry for trout with the rod, and it delights her. I think that would make George happy.

February 2001. The true history of the Delaware Special that I bought from George Maurer in 1996 is a bit of a mystery. I do remember that it was a two-piece that was flamed in a tortoise-shell design. I treasured the rod for its all-around versatility on my home water, the South Platte River. The Delaware Special cast a wonderful dry fly and could hold its own when I had to nymph fish. Some cane rod aficionados don't like to talk about nymph fishing in the same breath as bamboo, but where I live you have to do it once in awhile, whether you like to or not. At those times it's nice to have a rod that will rise to the occasion. And the simple truth is that I've never had a cane rod that was as good a dry fly rod and nymph rod as the Delaware Special. I don't know what the magic ingredient was.

George insists that the rod was 7 feet 9 inches long, and I don't question that, but it fished like an 8-footer. I like rods that fish big. I can say that my Delaware Special was a bit of a proto-type, too. It had 001 for a serial number, and there were a few minor problems along the way that we ironed out.

"The names got switched in there at the beginning. I think that I'd given John [Gierach] some rods to test, and you must have gotten hold of them, too. He eventually ended up with an 8-footer out of it that I called the Trout Bum, but one of those ear-lier prototypes you guys tried said Delaware Special on it, I think," George said.

Maurer said that the Delaware Special was a two-piece 7-foot 9-inch rod for a 5-weight line that had been influenced by a Payne taper.

"It kind of started when I was looking at an 8-foot, 5-weight Payne and said to myself, If I tweak this and do that and turn it into a 7-foot 9-inch rod, I think I can get a really nice rod. That was my intention," he said.

I was fishing the rod on the South Platte River in Elevenmile Canyon a number of years later on a very cold late winter day. There had been a rumor of trout rising to midges, so I'd headed up to the river. All I caught was a bunch of ice in the guides and a pair of half-frozen hands. I was trying to break the ice out of the tip-top guide when I snapped the tip. I knew that I should have put the rod down and warmed the ice a bit with my hand before I tried to remove it, but I just didn't and I paid the price. I hated myself, but also knew there was a spare tip.

Eventually I glued a one-size-larger tip-top on to the broken tip. I didn't lose more than an inch of length, and the slightly shorter tip cast well enough. A year or so after the tip broke, the rod developed a minor ferrule problem and I sent it back to George. A few weeks later he called.

"I could fix this, but I've really learned a lot more about making rods since I built this one. Why I don't I just make you a new rod?" he asked.

At the time I had the jones for a 6-weight rod that could handle bigger Montana water. I knew about George's Rocky Mountain Trout Bum, which is essentially a beefed up version of the 5-weight Trout Bum that he developed for John Gierach. I asked him if he'd mind making me a three-piece Rocky Mountain Trout Bum. Within a few months it arrived on my doorstep ready for the Yellowstone River or bass fishing in Nebraska.

But I still sometimes miss the Delaware Special. I know that George makes rods with more knowledge now, but I liked the pioneer outlook that first Delaware Special brought to the river. It was a kind of I-can-do-anything attitude that was refreshing in a world of more and more specialized bamboo fly rods.

Nowadays, the Delaware Special has been supplanted by the Rocky Mountain Special in George's catalog.

"The Rocky Mountain Special is also a 7-foot 9-inch rod for a 5-weight, but it is a different style taper. But I kept the Delaware Special taper, so I could still build it again if someone wanted it," he said.

Maybe I'm just getting old, but I'm glad he kept the taper.

April 2001. I was out on the lawn casting the Rocky Mountain Trout Bum in anticipation of an upcoming largemouth bass expedition to Nebraska in June. I plan to break it in on the bass and then take it up to the Montana big water in September.

The rod is fitted with an uplocking Bellinger reel seat with the western grip that hides a pocket for the reel foot under the cork. There is a knurled Bellinger winding check that sets off the cinnamon wraps. The single stripping guide is an original Mildrum. REC had recently bought Mildrum, and the scuttlebutt is that the design of the stripper has been changed a bit. The blued ferrules are Super-Z style from Bailey Woods. The Pacific Bay snake guides are titanium coated. The cane is flamed to a pleasing darked amber that nicely offsets the three-and-three node work.

On the grass the rod is a cannon with a heart. It can really cast the line, but I get the sense that if need be I'll be able to delicately work a dry fly close-in. Still, the rod effortlessly casts out to 60 feet. A quick single or double haul sends the leader to 75 feet and then 80 feet. I'm using a 6-weight Long Belly fly line from Royal Wulff that George recommended, but earlier a 6-weight double taper cast just fine, as did a 7-weight weight forward line. The Long Belly will be my trout line on this rod and the 7-weight forward with a short leader will probably end up turning over the clunkier bass bugs in Nebraska.

"The taper on the Trout Bum is a mix of a number of things, but the greatest influence is the Young tapers. It's not an exact copy of anything that Young did, but it falls into the style of taper he made," Maurer said.

Maurer said that it still scares him to call it a semiparabolic taper because people think that the rod will be hard to cast.

"I just hand them the rod and don't say anything. They cast, they smile, and they say, I want it," he said.

Just cast it! That's what I say . . . because you never know anything about a rod until you do.

CHAPTER TWELVE

Green River Rodmakers

December 1996. Running into Robert Gorman at the International Fly Tackle Dealer Show last September was among the better things that happened to me there. I won't even try to describe what it's like to wander through row after endless row of new and improved high-tech fly-fishing gizmos other than to say that it isn't always pretty. Stumbling onto Robert and his Green River booth, which was thoughtfully stocked with a number of his sweet casting bamboo fly rods, may have saved my life.

Robert immediately saw that I was suffering from fly-fishing show overdose and jammed one of his Mettowee series impregnated cane rods into my hand. He gently guided me to the casting pool and quietly said, "Try this one."

I thanked him and headed out to the casting line. After a few false casts I started to feel that sanity was coming back into my world. Bob had handed me his 6-foot Mettowee two-piece rod

Robert Gorman

for a 4-weight line. It's the quintessential little upland stream rod. Before I knew it, I was down on one knee and casting the rod the way I would if I were actually fishing a small stream.

It's a good sign when a rod compels you to cast it the way it should be fished. I began picking out the little bits of yarn left floating on the pool when the graphite rod casters tailed their loops trying to "put one out of the park" and aimed delicate little casts at them. The Mettowee was in its element, making the short- to medium-range highly accurate casts. Once in awhile, in between double hauls, one of the graphite people glanced down at my kneeling figure with a look of disdain. I kept my own council.

A few months later Robert sent me two Mettowee series rods, a 6-footer and 7-footer, both for a 4-weight line, to test under less stressful conditions. I started with the 6-footer and was struck once again by how I found myself wanting to crouch down into my small-stream fishing mode. The rod has a lively dry fly action that stays up toward the tip even on casts out to 50 feet. It's no easy feat to build that kind of response into a 6-foot rod for a 4-weight line.

I cast both double-taper and weight forward 4-weight lines on the rod. The weight forward line worked the best. With the application of a single or double haul, the rod cast easily out to 75 feet, which is far beyond the zone of practical use for a rod of this size. In addition, the rod made an admirable roll cast even with the weight forward line. More than anything, what I wanted to do with this rod was get down low, tuck my elbow in close to my side, and make the kind of highly accurate tight looped casts in the 15- to 35-foot range that so often comprise a day of small-stream angling for me.

The 7-foot Mettowee mirrored the 6-footer in looks, but its personality was clearly unique. It was a bit tippier than the 6-footer, which meant it could cast even tighter loops. On the distance end you could add about 10 feet or so to the 6-foot rod's performance in every category. Once again, the 7-footer cast best with a weight forward line.

When making extremely short casts with just the first 5 feet of fly line out, I found that both rods performed well if I remembered to assertively load them by stopping the rod on the backcast. Accuracy in very short casting ranges was excellent.

Although Gorman will gladly craft a custom cane rod to any specification or build a graphite rod as part of his Green River operation, he's the first to admit a personal affinity for New England's small streams and the cane rods that make fishing them a joy. That affinity stands out clearly in the Mettowee series. There are four one-piece rods in the 6- and 6½-foot range for 3-weight and 4-weight lines, along with the very short one-piece Brush

Rod category, which includes 4½-foot to 5-foot rods for 4-weight and 5-weight lines. More standard two-piece rods range from 6 to 8 feet, with three-piece rods available from 7 to 8 feet. Of the nineteen listed rods in the Mettowee series, there are just two 8-foot rods, the rest are 7½ feet or smaller.

"I don't like making anything bigger than an 8-foot rod for a 5-weight line because it just starts to get too heavy. It's especially true with my cane rods because I make them with the swelled butt, which adds some weight," said Gorman.

Gorman has been building bamboo fly rods for twenty years. He went into full-time rod building eight years ago when he formed Green River Rodmakers in Brattleboro, Vermont.

"I was originally an architect. On one of my escapes from New York, I stopped in at the Thomas & Thomas rod-building shop right after they moved into Sewell Dunton's old shop in Greenfield, Massachusetts. I had on my tasseled loafers and three-piece suit and sort of felt like an idiot, but I knew the second I walked in there that I wanted to build fly rods. It was a great, great moment for me. I really understood the world at that point," Gorman said.

Gorman became friends with both Thomas Dorsey and Thomas Maxwell at Thomas & Thomas. It was Tom Maxwell who eventually introduced him to master rod builder Sam Carlson. Gorman became Carlson's apprentice in 1973.

"After I met Sam was when I really started to learn how to make rods. I was an apprentice from 1973 to 1976. I was the only apprentice he ever had," Gorman said.

Today, Robert Gorman is known by fly fishers for the high quality of his cane rods, which feature a unique impregnation process.

"I impregnate my rods with varnish, not plastic or polymers like most impregnated rods. The plastics just add weight to the rod, but by impregnating with varnish I keep the weight close to what it would be if I'd just applied three coats of varnish to the outside of the rod," Gorman said.

The rods are impregnated to make them essentially mainte-nance-free.

"The varnish goes through the rod blank in the impregnation process, so there's always going to be varnish coming out. If you get a nick or a hook gouge, all you have to do is take a cloth and polish it. The heat caused by the rubbing will bring more varnish to the surface, so you'll always have a polished rod that never has to be refinished," Gorman said.

Gorman also said that with a varnish impregnation, rather than a heavier polymer, the action of the rod isn't "deadened" like in other impregnated rods.

"The rods are really alive. They haven't lost anything; in fact, they might have gained a little bit because they're a bit stiffer," he said.

That extra touch of stiffness can be especially nice in lighter line-weight small rods, which can tend toward medium or even slower actions. Gorman flames the cane for his rods to a uniform dark brown. It is then milled into splines and glued into blanks with nodes matched on every other spline to form a traditional staggering pattern of three on three.

"I make all the prototypes on the planing form and then go to the milling machine once I figure things out. I usually end up touching up about half of the milled blanks on the hand-planing forms. I use a 1930s milling machine that Tom Maxwell got me from the Detroit area. I had the original Hawes milling machine. It was the first one that he made for the Leonard Company, but I could never get it to work right, so I got this newer one," Gor-man said.

The actual impregnation process is accomplished by putting the rod blanks in a cold bath of the varnish and resins for approx-imately ten days, depending on weather and humidity. Gorman always adds an extra blank, or "suicide stick," into the bath so that he can periodically cut into it to see how the impregnation process is progressing.

When the impregnation process is complete, he removes the rod blanks from the bath and allows them to dry for several days. The blanks are then dipped briefly into the cold bath again and "cooked" for a few hours in the same oven used to temper the raw cane.

"After the blank has been impregnated, if you take a piece of flannel and rub, it glows like a varnished rod. And the interesting thing is that you can bring that glow up for the life of the rod by just rubbing it out. You can make it look practically new," Gorman said.

Gorman said that the impregnation process lengthens the time it takes to build a single rod, but that he can impregnate a number of blanks at a time.

Once the impregnation process is complete, the blanks are ferruled with the new Bailey Woods–tapered Super-Z ferrules, which are a bit shorter than other Super-Z's. The ferrules are the only component of a Gorman rod that isn't made in his Brattleboro shop.

"I make the reel seats from burled maple that I collect right around here. I hand rub them with tung oil to bring out the grain. The nickel silver hardware is all made right here, too," he said.

Gorman's reel seats are among the finest I have seen. The mortise work on some features is what Gorman calls his church window detail, where the mortise comes gracefully to an arch on the upper end and forms what looks like an old church window.

The cork grips on the lighter rods are "short, very slim cigars." The grip on $7\frac{1}{2}$-foot and longer rods goes to a modified Payne-style or western grip with a hooded cap concealed in the grip. Typically, the hardware consists of either upsliding or downsliding rings or ring and cap combinations for 4-weight and lighter rods. At 5-weight Gorman goes to uplocking screw lock hardware. The stripping guides are the fine and elegant Mildrum carbide type.

"I don't know what I'll do when I run out of these stripping guides. When Mildrum closed, I bought all that I could. I really like them. I do use agate occasionally on special orders, but it's expensive and can break," Gorman said.

The stripping guide, line guides, and ferrules are wrapped in green and tipped black.

"I put several coats of urethane on the wraps first and then put a final coat of epoxy over that. I don't want the epoxy to come into contact with the cane at all," Gorman said.

A ring-style hook keeper is positioned above the winding check midway through a green wrap, which is tipped black with two detached black tags. Two additional green wraps tipped in black are placed further up the butt to complete the signature wrap.

The rods are inscribed "Green River," followed by a three-digit code. The first two digits of the code indicate the rod's length in feet and inches. The final digit indicates recommended line weight. Another four-digit code occurs after the three-digit code. In this code the first two digits signify Gorman's age when the rod was built. The last two digits are the rod number for that year.

"All in all I see the whole process of building a cane rod as being a lot like making a violin. Why else would you do it, if not to come out with something that is a craft and a work of art," Gorman said and then, with a twinkle in his eye, added, "The Buddha would call this right livelihood, and I agree, but it's a heck of a way to make a living."

It appears as though Gorman's "right living" makes for some righteous fly-fishing rods. The Buddha would be pleased.

April 2001. "I just wanted to go back to making a classic bamboo rod," Robert Gorman said about his Rawson Place Signature Rods.

Gorman said that his Mettowee series of impregnated rods continue to be available, but the Rawson Place rods, which he began offering as a two-piece premier signature rod more than four years ago, have become quite popular. The Rawson Place rods feature a varnish finish, vintage agate stripper guides (not agatetine), antique bronze guides from the 1930s, and gorgeous reel seats with handcrafted nickel silver hardware very similar to those that grace the Mettowee series. The ferrules are the truncated Swiss style.

"The switch to varnished rods has been pretty dramatic in the past three or four years. I'd say I sell 60 to 70 percent varnished rods now, even though I tell people when they order a rod that the impregnated models are still absolutely maintenance-free and will polish up to a luster just about the same as a varnished rod. They still opt for the classic model rods anyway," Gorman said.

Gorman said that although he is selling mostly varnished rods, now he has incorporated some of what he learned from impregnating rods into the varnish finish.

"I liked what I learned from impregnating rods—things such as limiting the amount of maintenance that a rod needs so that it can compete favorably with graphite just on that level. I varnish the rods using parts of the process that I learned from impregnation. Some of the varnish really does go into the rod with this process. It doesn't go in 100 percent, like it does with impregnation, but it does go inside. With a dipped rod you just put varnish on the surface. I've had to formulate my own varnish for what I do now," he said.

Rawson Place rods, which were named after a place where Gorman lived, come in two- or three-piece models in 6- to 8-foot lengths with two tips. The Mettowee series is also available in two- and three-piece models in 6- to 8-foot lengths with two tips, and the unique one-piece Brush Rods in $4\frac{1}{2}$- to $6\frac{1}{2}$-foot lengths.

As is always the case when I talk with Robert Gorman, he waxes poetic toward the end of the conversation.

"You know, it still is right livelihood. If I wasn't so slow or could figure out a faster way of working, I might actually be able to make a living at this, too," he said and then laughed the kind of deep belly laugh you'd expect from Buddha.

CHAPTER THIRTEEN

Eden Cane, Ltd.

August 1999. Jeff Wagner, the talented rod builder from Parma Heights, Ohio, and I occasionally talk on the telephone. We usually start off raving about rods and rod builders, but we almost always end up pumping each other for information about what the trout are hitting in our respective parts of the country. I've always thought that that's the perfect progression for any good telephone conversation.

The last time we spoke Jeff suggested that I check out a Canadian rodmaker named Bernard Ramanauskas. Ramanauskas is the rod builder version of what we'd call a young gun in the guide business. He's been making rods for only the past few years, but his work has caught the eye of a number of cane rod aficionados. One admirer is Len Codella at Heritage Sporting Collectibles. Codella has featured Ramanauskas's new rods, which sell under the name of Eden Cane, Ltd., in the past several issues of his catalog.

Bernard Ramanauskas

PHOTO COURTESY OF
MR. ROGER HARRISON

The Ramanauskas rods are different from the majority of cane rods being built in North America for several reasons. Most important, Ramanauskas builds nodeless rods. For those of you unfamiliar with nodeless cane rod construction, it means that the node, or growth joint of the bamboo, is removed from the bamboo after it has been split. Once the node is removed, the strip is then spliced back together and glued. The bamboo strip is then planed into a triangular spline.

In a traditionally constructed cane rod, the nodes remain part of the strip. The nodes typically create "bends" in the strip that must be straightened. After straightening, the nodes are then gently sanded or planed before the strip is milled and/or planed into the triangular spline. Nodeless construction usually requires less straightening of the bamboo strips than traditional rod construction.

In addition to his nodeless construction, Ramanauskas often uses semihollow construction techniques pioneered on the West Coast when he builds 8-foot and longer rods designed for 5-weight and heavier fly lines.

I always get excited when the UPS man shows up with a box or tube that unmistakably holds a fly rod. Bernard Ramanauskas's rods came neatly packaged in a box from Len Codella. It held a nifty little blond three-piece 7-footer based on a Gillum taper for a 4- or 5-weight line and a sweet caramel-colored three-piece 7-foot 3-inch rod for a 4- or 5-weight line based on a Garrison taper. The first thing I looked for when I uncased the rods was the nodeless construction. And sure enough there were no nodes on the rods. There were numerous, almost invisible, angled "splices" where the nodes had been removed from each spline and then glued back together. It was the first time I'd ever seen a nodeless rod.

I grabbed my reels with the 4-weight and 5-weight lines on them and hustled down to the local park to give each rod a whirl.

I began with a double-taper 4-weight line on the Garrison-inspired 7-foot 3-inch rod. With this line weight it cast nicely, with just a few feet of line out from the tip-top. As I false cast more line out, I liked what I saw and felt. The fly line remained smooth with very few shock waves in it. It's been my experience with cane rods that a good caster can dampen shock waves in the line when false casting most any rod, but what I like to see is an action that dampens the waves without me having to think about. This was one of those rods. It cast smoothly and effortlessly within my optimal fishing range of 15 to 50 feet. I cranked it out to 65 feet without a haul and managed about 75 feet with a crisp single haul. I didn't ask the rod for anything more in the distance department because that's all I could ever see myself wanting it to do, but I am sure if called upon and double hauled the rod would do 85 feet in a pinch.

After the distance work I spent some time casting to dandelions. The rod felt good in the hand, and I didn't have to fight it to put the fly where I wanted it to go. The rod is pretty much an all-around smoothie. I also cast it with a 5-weight double-taper line. It performed admirably, but the rod deflected just a tad more than I like. Nonetheless, a 5-weight line is well within the casting parameters of this rod. It's always so personal.

I took a moment to admire the rod before I moved on to the 7-footer. The Briar burl reel seat is mortised to accept the reel foot. There is a nickel silver butt plate and nickel silver sliding band. The slightly modified western-style grip hides a hooded cap under the cork for the reel foot. The exquisite nickel silver cork check is laminated with reel seat wood, as is the winding check at the front of the grip. An Eden Cane logo and hand-printed serial number appear on the butt section of the rod above the Pacific Bay hook keeper.

The silk windings around the hook keeper and snake guides closely match the reel seat wood and are tipped in claret. The stripping guide is a Daryll Whitehead agate matched to the blond bamboo of the rod. The signature wrap is two windings of the body color of the guide wrap, then two windings of the tipping color, followed by two more windings of the body color. The nickel silver ferrules are Super-Z's from Bailey Woods.

The rod is very nicely finished with a polyurethane that doesn't feel sticky to the touch, as other polyurethane finishes sometimes do.

I next turned my attention to the 7-footer with the Gillum-influenced taper. I started out with a double taper 4-weight line but switched over to a 5-weight forward, which cast close-in rather nicely. The rod has a real sweet spot for casting to average fishing distances of 15 to 50 feet and goes out nicely to 65 feet without hauling. It's a surprisingly strong rod when double hauled. I managed a 75-foot cast with my typically uncoordinated double haul on my first attempt and had the line out an additional 5 feet when I concentrated on what I was doing. That's pretty good for a 7-foot rod.

Directing the fly to a target is close to effortless at normal fishing ranges and immediately brings to mind the rod's possibilities as a pocket water instrument.

In appearance the rod is very similar in cosmetic design and components to the 7-foot 3-inch rod, with the exception of the caramel-colored cane and darker maple root burl reel seat with matching guide wraps. Tipping is black.

The first question to come to mind when you talk with Bernard Ramanauskas is "Why make nodeless rods?" Although nodeless rods have been made and sold, most notably as the Sans Noeud limited edition of twenty rods by Thomas & Thomas in 1981, their popularity with North American rod builders has been limited to a rod here and there by Garrison, Dickerson, and a smattering of other builders.

Garrison's only attempt at a nodeless rod was built by cutting the nodes out perpendicular to the grain of the spline and then butting the two pieces together. The Thomas & Thomas nodeless rods were cut at an angle to the grain of the spline and then the scarfed sections were joined. Ramanauskas nodeless rods are made along the lines of the Thomas & Thomas rods with scarfed and joined splices. The "splices" or "joints" in the Thomas & Thomas rods were staggered in a three-on-three pattern. Unlike other builders of nodeless rods, Ramanauskas does not stagger the joints.

"I build nodeless rods for three reasons," Ramanauskas said. "Having the liberty to remove damaged or marred sections of the bamboo is a big aesthetic concern to me. I want to make a clean rod. Besides, I have very little faith in nodes. I don't like the stitching effect that occurs when the nodes are staggered on the finished rod, and I don't like the idea that you're building a rod that hinges all over the place. That's basically what a node is. It a place where the rod flexes differently. Finally, and this is purely selfish, I loathe having to straighten splines with nodes in them. If I had to do it day in and day out I wouldn't be building rods."

Ramanauskas maintains that eliminating nodes in the rod helps standardize the rod-building process for him.

"It allows you to assembly line the process during the splitting-out stage. You just can't do that when you're splitting a culm for a traditionally constructed rod. Once you've figured out the tricks, getting a culm to the point where you can start making a taper is grunt work. All the mystery is taken out and it's straight ahead," he said.

Ramanauskas parts out between six and ten culms of bamboo at a time, which keeps him supplied with rod-building material for three to four months.

"Because of the way I split, sort, and splice the cane, the quality is assured. Once I'm done, my quality considerations are over. I really look at this as the grunt part of the job. I do it all at once so I have to do it only twice a year," he said.

Ramanauskas points out that when he splits and splices material for nodeless rods he keeps the configuration of the original culm for each spline. When a node is removed, the spline is faithfully rejoined in its original configuration.

"Once the splitting and sorting is done, I get to what I consider the art phase. The joy for me is seeing the personality of each culm dictate the taper of the rod. I split the material out, sit down with it for an afternoon, and decide what I'm going to make based on what I see," Ramanauskas said.

Ramanauskas considers the "finishing" stage of his rod building to include building the blank and everything that comes after it.

"Once I split out the material, everything after that is aimed toward the finish. I try to keep my ego out of the rod building and focus my attention on the rods themselves," he said.

Ramanauskas uses a milling machine to initially bevel the splines, but hand planes each piece for the final fit. In regard to tapers, Ramanauskas said he doesn't have any single dominant influence.

"I try to pick a taper appropriate to the specific rod I'm building. I do have loyalties to some builders, though. For sheer brain power, I'd go with Dickerson. For interesting tapers, I like Gillum. I think Paul Young was wonderful. And surprisingly, I think Garrison was overrated, with the exception of two tapers. What you have to understand is that there was so much cross-pollination. F. E. Thomas is just wonderful if you want a Payne- or Leonard-style rod. He seemed to do a better job of what everybody else was trying to do at the time in terms of what you might call slow-tipped rods," Ramanauskas said.

I asked Ramanauskas about the opinion held by some rod builders and bamboo aficionados that nodeless rods are weaker than traditionally constructed cane rods.

"I think there was a time when a nodeless rod might have been weaker where it was joined, but I think the same thing can be said for all the rods in general at the time. The culprit was the adhesives, and weaknesses occurred whether the rod was nodeless or not. You could say that adhesives destroyed Gillum's career. He was a pretty hot rod builder, but his rods delaminated and that was the end of it for him. He folded his shop and said no more," Ramanauskas said.

Ramanauskas has spent considerable time doing in-house experimentation on rod adhesives.

"I've probably spent more time on adhesives than anything else. The outcome in a rod depends entirely on the quality of the adhesives and the prep work devoted to their use. Modern adhesives are like towing a 200-pound trailer with a two-ton hitch. They are very good. The trick is that you have to know what your glue can and cannot do," he said.

Ramanauskas stands by his research on adhesives and simply states that his rods are the proof.

"If you look carefully at my rods, you'll notice that my node-less joints are not staggered. That's my trademark in a rod. I do it because I can and it comes in handy when building semihollow rods. In a small way, I also do it to prove a point. I'm able to do it because adhesives are just that good nowadays. On my personal demonstration rods I have a nodeless section 2 inches from the rod tip. I don't do this on the rods I sell, but I did it on my own to prove a point. If something is going to go wrong with a joint, that's where it will happen. I've put those demo rods through hell and back, and I have not had a single problem. So the weakness argument for nodeless rods is specious at best," he said.

Ramanauskas estimated that the average two-piece 7-foot nodeless rod that he builds has about eighty splices where nodes have been removed, if you include both tips in the count.

Ramanauskas makes trout rods in various lengths from 6 to 9 feet for 2-weight to 8-weight lines. They are available in two, three, and four pieces. Bamboo comes in blond, caramel, and tiger torch tones.

"The tiger torch is very dark, but I burn only the surface of the cane. I don't go deep. There's an argument that adding a bit of carbon to a rod makes it faster and crisper. That may or may not be true. I think it affects the nodes, but if you remove the nodes, it's a moot point anyway," he said.

Eden rods are dipped in a polyurethane finish that was designed to protect gymnasium floors. A positive aspect of the polyurethane finish is that it doesn't degrade as quickly as spar varnish in ultraviolet light. Ramanauskas has also developed a special polymer formula finish with a plastics company in Vancouver, British Columbia, for guide wraps that won't photo deteriorate.

"This stuff is like liquid steel. It markedly reduces ferrule wrap and stripping guide cracking. I haven't had a thread separate with the stuff yet, and I can't see it ever happening. I know this is something rodmakers have been trying to solve for years and I just stumbled on to it," Ramanauskas said.

I was impressed with the simple, elegant lines of the reel seats on the Eden Cane rods that I cast.

"I have a little mini-warehouse with about eighty varieties of wood for reel seats. I find that Danish oil works best as a finish on most of them. I have this thing about the reel seat. I don't want it to be a platform for the rod. The reel seat is really just a glorified clamp, and I feel dishonest about having all this knurling and stuff on it. It looks like it doesn't belong to the rod. I don't want the reel seat to be the focus of the rod. The rod should stand on its own and not be justified by the reel seat," he said.

In addition to laminating reel seat woods on the cork check and winding check on some rods, Ramanauskas also laminates the front of the grip on selected rods with a fletching of reel seat wood, which produces a swelled butt that matches the reel seat and wraps.

A final note on Eden rods is the meaning of the serial numbers. The first two digits designate rod length in feet and inches, the second two digits indicate the size of the first ferrule. A dash after the first four digits is followed by the size of the second ferrule in a three-piece rod. A lowercase letter in the serial number indicates a taper influenced by another rod builder. An *e* means Garrison, a *g* Gillum, and a *d* Dickerson. If no lowercase letter appears, it indicates a taper more strongly influenced by Ramanauskas's own ideas.

"The serial number is modeled after Dickerson's. It gives the buyer a little information, and you can roughly figure line weights for the rod by the ferrule sizes," said Ramanauskas.

Rod cases are hard-bodied tubes covered with Cordora nylon cloth. Ramanauskas had them specially designed. They are vented and have a permanently built-in inner cloth lining, which is compartmentalized for the rod sections.

"I put a lot of thought into the rod case. It has perforations on the top and bottom that take care of shifts in humidity. You don't have to dry the rod before putting it in the case. The built-in sock is durable and easy to use. It's kind of a no-brainer way to make sure the rod gets stored right," he said.

In a number of ways Ramanauskas has found his way out to the cutting edges of modern cane rod building. He challenges many traditionally held rod-building notions—right down to the design of the rod case.

"The whole craft right now is seeing a revival in popularity, and we are beginning to see the next stage in the development of cane rods. I think you'd be hard-pressed to go through rod archives and find stuff that compares with the work of today's best rodmakers. I think knowing where the craft came from is important. I also think fostering that heritage is important, too, but it can be exceedingly limiting if you buy into the idea that there's only one way to do something. Your work is going to suffer. You constantly have to reinvent the wheel," Ramanauskas said.

March 2001. Dusty Sprague and I have arrived at a high-plains reservoir in eastern Colorado on a god-awful windy day. The plan was to try to catch a few early season northern pike on the fly. At this time Dusty is the only certified Federation of Fly Fishers (FFF) master fly casting instructor in the state of Colorado. I figure that if anyone can blast a cast through the wind Dusty can. He has come equipped with some sort of lightning-fast 9-foot graphite fly rod fitted with a shiny brass-colored saltwater fly reel.

I have taken this opportunity to further test the prototype of a three-piece 8½-foot bass/steelhead 7-weight bamboo fly rod that Bernard Ramanauskas sent to me a few weeks ago. I'd been whining to him about how I was trying to find the cosmic bass rod for my annual Nebraska bass-fishing foray with John Gierach. Bernard accepted the thinly veiled challenge and suggested that he might like to give a bass/steelhead rod taper a whirl. He asked if I'd want to get in on the initial field tests.

I volunteered without hesitation, even though I have a full understanding of the perils of being the test pilot for a newly designed fly rod. I am a veteran of this work, and I can tell you that it's no fun having 60 or 70 feet of fly line in the air and suddenly experiencing a catastrophic loop failure. Everything goes into slow motion, and you hear your pals yelling, "Pull up, pull up!" and then the large, heavily weighted woolly bugger hits you in the head. You fight to keep from blacking out, knowing that a face plant into the icy reservoir or river is certain death. It's dangerous work for sure, but someone has to do it.

The Ramanauskas rod does look up to the task. The bamboo is uniformly dark—flamed almost to a molasses color. There is a nice agate stripping guide. Wraps are black. The 6½-inch cork grip is a western-style design with a hidden pocket under the cork for the reel foot. Bernard's signature reel seat check and winding check, which are characteristically laminated in the reel seat spacer wood, are in beautiful evidence. The reel seat wood itself is nicely figured and mortised with a sliding band. I've already suggested that the band might be a bit lightweight for a butt-kicking bass rod, and Bernard will adjust it to an uplocking version after the initial tests.

The rod cast like a rocket when I took it for a spin on the grass before the trip. It's tippy, tight, and built to romp. I cast the full 7-weight forward Cortland 444 with a single haul. A double haul had me shooting into the backing. Shorter casts came off without a hitch, although I didn't have a fly on the leader. The acid test, of course, is how the rod does with a big, gooey, soaking wet bunny fly, or a heavily weighted woolly bugger, or a bulky wind-resistant deer hair popper.

For high plains pike fishing I decided on a 5-foot straight 30-pound test leader with a black-and-red bunny fly looped on the end. We decided to work the rocky dam face first. It was a bit out of the wind but offered all the normal annoyances associated with fishing along a dam. Backcasts had to be high. Too much line on the forward cast might inadvertently hit the water's surface. It is a situation custom-made for shooting line, and Bernard's rod accomplished that with aplomb.

We worked the entire dam face without a strike and moved out on to the wind-swept flats on the south side of the reservoir. The rod rocketed the fly line nicely through a strong crosswind without much drift at all. It had no difficulty whatsoever turning over the now thoroughly soaked and weighty bunny fly. Midway across the flats we still had not gotten a strike.

We both got that sinking feeling that comes when conditions are just not right. I took the water temperature. It was in the low 40s, which is not propitious for catching pike on the fly. Still, we forged ahead, casting our way around the reservoir until we were full bore into a stiff head wind. I told Dusty I wanted to see what the rod would do in the wind and then I'd be perfectly happy to make my way back to the truck. Under the most trying conditions it performed admirably. I was actually able to turn the fly over directly into the wind and make a forward cast of maybe 35 or 40 feet. It was big wind, and the rod cut through it.

On the way back to the truck, I asked Dusty to hand me his fly rod. I hefted both the rods and was surprised to note that there was very little difference in weight between Dusty's 9-foot graphite rod for a 7-weight fly line outfitted with the somewhat heavier saltwater reel and my 8½-foot bamboo rod. The bamboo rod actually felt a bit lighter, which surprised both of us.

All and all, Bernard's rod did okay on its first fishing trip. I'd have liked to see what it could do with a decent-sized northern pike, but that will have to wait.

April 2001. Bernard seems pleased with the results of the bass rod's initial tests. He said the rod taper is one of his own designs and that he now uses all his own taper ideas on his dry fly and wet fly series trout rods, too. He's also converted to a more traditional and time-tested spar varnish finish. The rods are dipped and hand polished between numerous coats. In addition, all reel seats on Eden Cane rods now use impregnated burl.

As with all rodmakers, the work, the learning, and the innovation go on.

CHAPTER FOURTEEN

F. D. Lyons
Rod Company

May 1999. I let out a palpable sigh of relief when I got my hands on the fly rod Dwight Lyons had sent me. It was no easy task to receive the rod. The little Colorado town I live in had just received 12 inches of rain in two days. That may not sound like a lot to some of you, but our average annual precipitation is only 16 inches, so it was a big deal for us. Floodwaters rampaged down Williams Canyon, blew out a culvert on the way to Fountain Creek, jumped into Canon Avenue, and crashed through Soda Springs Park. The post office was inaccessible. My telephone was out.

Within a few days the post office set up an emergency mail distribution center at Town Hall. I made my way through the receding waters to see if the rod, which Dwight had sent several days before, had made it. When the postmaster walked toward me holding the big white PVC tube that so many rodmakers use to ship their precious cargo, I was a happy camper. I was even happier when I got home and broke the seal on the mailing tube.

Dwight Lyons

Nestled in the Styrofoam popcorn was a slender aluminum tube capped with brass on both ends.

When I slipped the rod from the khaki-colored rod bag, it was clear that the ghost of H. L. Leonard was lurking in the three-piece 3½-ounce, 8-foot bamboo rod that I held in my hands. The tip-off was the graceful Leonard-style cigar grip that tapered all the way to the nickel silver hooded butt cap. A somewhat wider-than-usual sliding ring encircled the continuous cork handle. The nickel silver winding check at the top of the grip gave way to a signature wrap consisting of a wide burgundy silk winding with a ring-style hook keeper in the center, followed by narrow windings of rust, antique gold, and very dark maroon over the slightly swelled butt.

The nickel silver stripping guide was a classic old-style low-bridge agate wrapped in burgundy silk. The ferrule was a waisted (also referred to as step-down) type in the Leonard tradition. Wraps on the male ferrule of the midsection and tip section mirrored the signature wrap at the butt. The snake guides all had elegant burgundy wraps that contrasted gorgeously with the blond cane characterized by three-by-three node spacing. The node work was compact and artful.

A few days later, when I took the rod to a somewhat dry, grassy town park that hadn't got hammered by the floods, I couldn't shake the thought that this is a rod for the backcountry. It had pack trip written all over it. The rod possessed a light, airy character that was accentuated by the all-cork grip, lightweight hooded butt cap, and sliding ring. The narrow-diameter aluminum rod tube capped in brass is compact and thrifty.

I took a Peerless 1½ and a Hardy LRH reel, both outfitted with double-taper 5-weight lines, with me for the rod test, but it was clear that this Lyons rod would be best paired with the lighter-weight Hardy LRH. That reel happened to have a Scientific Anglers Ultra-3 line on it that suited the rod perfectly.

I deviated from my normal rod-testing agenda, where I make short casts first, and found myself cranking out line on the initial false casts. I just couldn't help it after I felt the first pulse of life enter the cane as the line went out through the guides. It was the silky smooth kind of feeling that can only come from a rod endowed with a fuller action.

Some casters might say the rod is a bit on the slow side, but I think that's a one-dimensional description that on some level compares the rod with graphite. And my first rule of thumb with cane is to never compare it with any other rod-building material. One of the great pleasures of bamboo is that it handles a broad range of tapers and their resulting actions so well. I appreciate the so-called slower rods because I think they make me a better caster. Besides, they make for a sensuous fishing partner.

There was no doubt this rod could cast a line. The fly line romped out to 60 feet without hesitation, and a single, crisp double haul had the line out to 75 feet, which is well beyond my practical fishing range. The rod was capable of casting very tight, fluid loops with little effort on my part. It needed very little direction or management to deliver slack line casts, pile casts, reach casts, and curve casts. I understand that the caster is a big part of how any rod performs, but it's sure nice when the rod doesn't fight you. And this rod aimed to please.

I eventually got around to casting in the critical mid-distance range of 20 to 40 feet. The rod shines at these distances. Once again, the fuller action allowed a greater feel of what the rod could do and that helped me make wonderfully accurate casts with ease and expediency. It's the reason that I'm a bamboo nut. Needless to say, the rod performs well even at very close ranges.

The final pleasure came when I disassembled the rod and noted the pleasant "pop" when I pulled the ferrules apart. They came apart easily, but the fit was firm, strong, and perfect. It was so nice that I couldn't resist putting the rod together one more time just to feel the exquisite fit.

I called Dwight Lyons the next day. Once I got past mooning over how much I liked the rod, I asked him if there was indeed a Leonard connection.

"It's true I've been influenced by the Leonards and Paynes," he said.

Lyons said that the rod I'd cast had been modeled on the Leonard 50 taper.

"What I do is take a taper, graph it, and make some changes. It isn't exactly a Leonard taper when I'm done, but the influence is there. If I like a taper, I don't mind using it at all. That rod you cast has its origins in a taper that is close to one hundred years old. Those old rods had drop rings on them and cast beautifully," he said.

Lyons said that he has been strongly influenced by the Leonard 50s, the Leonard 38H, and some of the Payne tapers.

"Most recently I've been getting intrigued by the Garrisons because I've cast a few. Although I'm not really enamored by the way they are finished, the tapers are pretty good, at least on the ones I've cast," he said.

Lyons obtains the superlative finish on his rods with spar varnish and a dipping machine. He hand planes the bamboo for all of his rods.

Lyons didn't come to building cane rods by the standard route. His bamboo rod restorations and repairs have been recognized among bamboo aficionados for more than twenty years, but he didn't start building cane rods until 1991.

"I never fished before I got married in 1966. My father-in-law was a fisherman, and that's what got me started. We fished bait on fly rods then and got pretty deadly at it. After I did that for awhile, I started looking for something more challenging and decided to get into fly-fishing. Although my father-in-law had fly-fished, he wasn't really interested in teaching me, so I went down to the department store and bought an el cheapo fly-fishing outfit and taught myself to cast. As time went by, I started fiddling around with the equipment," he said.

Lyons said that he came across an article on bamboo rods in *Sports Afield* that was illustrated with photos of Payne and Gillum rods.

"I thought they were such great-looking rods that I started frequenting antique stores and second-hand stores where I found old bamboo rods. I brought them home, stripped them, and rewrapped them. It just kind of took off from there. Mostly I picked up low-end production rods, like Montagues and the occasional Granger. I'd fix them up and sell them. As I got more interested, I tried to duplicate and repair them as close to the originals as I could," he said.

Lyons's work has led him to numerous secondhand stores and sewing shops in search of old silk threads to match the original guide wraps on the rods he was restoring. When he found old rods that couldn't be restored, he salvaged the useable parts and saved them for future restorations.

"It's basically a scrounger's business. I've hunted down the old Tungsten snake guides and agate stripping guides. They're hard to get now, but I've put back a good supply. They do make agate stripper guides now, but they aren't the old smaller ones that you need to faithfully restore older rods. I can't convince anyone to make them the old way. They're all too large now. One manufacturer told me that these days people want the larger agate guides, and I told him I'm not doing *these days*," he said.

Lyons said that he's basically self-taught at rod restoration.

"I bought some old books, but there are surprisingly few that gave me any tips on what to do before Stuart Kirkfield's *The Fine Bamboo Rod—A Master's Secrets of Restoration and Repair* came out," he said.

Lyons went into full-time rod repair and restoration in 1988 after his job at Pacific Power and Light Company was eliminated in a downsizing move. That's when his long-time interest in building his own bamboo rods was rekindled.

"I think what really got me to thinking about building rods was the Garrison book. That was in 1976, and I split my first cane then and got everything ready to go, but I never got back to it until 1991," he said.

Lyons's interest and skill in restoring old cane is clearly evident in his rod building. He currently makes six models of cane rods.

"I settled on a line of rods from 7 to 8 feet. I make a 7-foot, 7½-foot, and 8-foot rod in a two-piece or three-piece for line weights 4 through 6. I think the action of these rods is more suitable to those line weights. If I go to lighter lines, I think the action gets a little too slow," he said.

Each of the models is fitted with oxidized step-down ferrules that Lyons machines himself out of 12 percent solid nickel silver stock.

"I make the ferrules to match those on the old Leonards. They're longer and I figure you have to make them that way because it was figured into the action of the rod," Lyons said.

The reel seat is a nickel silver cap and ring over a butternut wood spacer. An all-cork grip with pocketed butt cap and sliding band is also available. Lyons machines the sliding band and the winding check himself. The butt cap is from REC.

"I make the sliding band wider than most. The narrower ones probably look better, but they also dig into the cork," Lyons said.

Lyons uses $1/4$-inch cork rings on the grips because he believes they have fewer flaws than larger rings. He uses Mildrum snake guides on all models with a Perfection tip-top guide.

"People will be getting the old-style tungsten snake guides. I have a fair supply of them that I plan to use until I run out," he said.

Lyons heat treats the pre-embargo Tonkin cane a little but prefers that it retains its blond color, which contrasts nicely with the burgundy wraps. The serial number appears on the butt of the rod and consists of eight or nine digits. The first digit indicates the order in which the rod of that length for that year was produced. The second and third digits indicate the length. The number 280 would mean the second 8-foot rod of that model made in a given year. The fourth digit indicates the number of pieces, which is usually two or three. The fifth digit is the line weight. The next digit(s) indicates the month the rod was completed (one digit for January through September, two digits for October through December). The final two digits indicate the year the rod was built.

All rod models come with an extra tip, cloth partitioned bag and brass-capped aluminum rod tube.

"My wife makes all the rod bags—she's kind of the bag lady. She can just about duplicate any bag you want, which comes in handy in the restoration business. I think more people call her now than me," Lyons said.

Lyons said that he comes from a school of rod building where you make as many of the components for the rod as you can.

"I was taught rod building by Ed Hartzell. Myself and two other people from Portland got together one day and decided he was going to teach us to build rods. He agreed, so we met over at his house every Wednesday night for about a year. We pretty much went from A to Z when it comes to building a rod," he said.

It might be that Lyons took the longer road to rod building from a solid base in rod restoration, but that experience, coupled with the knowledge imparted to him from master rod builder Edwin Hartzell, shows in his work. Lyons's rod restoration work has allowed him to cast countless classic cane rods. The knowledge he has gained puts him in a position to capture the essence of the golden age of rod building in his work.

"I think if you buy a contemporary rod today you're getting a better rod than they built in the past, if only because our glues are better today. Of course, you're up against the mystique of the old rod builders when you make a statement like that, but today's rod builders really do make a great rod," Lyons said.

And I for one couldn't be happier that there are so many fine cane rod builders at work today. We may very well be in the second golden age of rod building.

CHAPTER FIFTEEN

The D. G. Schroeder Rod Company

September 1996. The first thing you'll notice when you pick up one of Don Schroeder's fly rods is a subtle "heft" near the handle. It's little more than a slight change in the rod's center of gravity, but that elusive difference puts it in the company of other fine fly rods, such as the Paynes, that are identifiable by the special "feel" they possess in the hand.

"The rod has a swelled butt, which means there is a lot of cane underneath the handle, and believe it or not, that does make the rod balance a lot better," Schroeder explained.

That extra cane under the handle may also account for what Schroeder refers to as the "reserve power" found in his fly rods.

"Most of my fishing here in Wisconsin is on spring creeks. It's a lot like Pennsylvania. Probably our biggest stream is no more than 50 feet across. You can jump over a lot of them. I found that even on the smaller spring creeks I sometimes needed to make

Don Schroeder

longer upstream casts to avoid disturbing a pool by wading through it. I wanted a rod where I could take out a few extra feet of line and cast it up to a small pool without disturbing anything. That's where the reserve power comes in. Sometimes the less waiting you do on a rising fish, the better," Schroeder said.

Schroeder's rods bear out his spring creek experiences. His 7$\frac{1}{2}$-foot for a 5-weight line passed all my standard rod tests. It casts well with as little as a foot or two of the fly line extended past the tip-top guide. Even more impressive was the uncanny accuracy of the rod out to 50, even 60, feet. What we're talking here is the ability to put a fly on a standard-size coffee cup saucer at 50 feet—and not every rod can do that.

Schroeder's idea of reserve power also means that you can pick up 40 or 50 feet of line effortlessly and immediately recast. That means you can get on risers fast without time-consuming line retrieval and endless false casts. It's the way Don likes it on his Wisconsin spring creeks.

The fact is that the 7½-foot rod that Don lent me casts cleanly, sweetly, and accurately to 60 feet without the application of a single or double haul. Needless to say, hauls added even more distance. In terms of pure comfort in casting, Schroeder's rod was one of the most impressive I've cast. You get the feeling that once you've loaded the rod the fly just wants to go where you point it. It's that simple.

The rod is also quite responsive. It throws S curves, right-hand curves, left-hand curves, and slack line casts with ease and authority. I didn't want to go home once I got the rod in my hand.

Like most builders of fine cane rods, Schroeder can build any rod a customer requests, but the majority of rods he builds represent his own bamboo fly rod philosophy.

"If someone calls me up and wants something special, I'll make it. I'm a custom rodmaker, but what I think happens is you develop a kind of standard line of rods that come to identify you. If you have all these different style rods and wraps and reel seats, all of a sudden it isn't your rod anymore. It's just a bunch of components put together," Schroeder said.

Schroeder's rods are characterized by a simple elegance. Reel seats come in two styles. Shorter rods in lighter line weights feature a nickel silver sliding band reel seat with a mortised walnut insert. The cork handle is a classic cigar shape. Heavier rods, roughly 7½-foot, 5-weights and up, utilize hardened aluminum uplocking reel seats with a California Claro walnut insert. The cork handle is a Payne style (also known as western grip) with the characteristic hooded cap concealed in the grip. Schroeder makes all his reel seat hardware from scratch.

"I've had that aluminum uplocking reel seat from the beginning. A lot of the older rods used aluminum for reel seats. Payne used it. I've never liked the way nickel silver gets that gold tarnish with age. I taught myself how to run the metal lathe, and I sat down and built reel seats until I got something I really liked. Now I'm known for that reel seat," Schroeder said.

Schroeder also hand machines the winding checks and ferrule plugs for his rods. "I make everything on the rod except the ferrules and line guides," he said.

Schroeder uses the always reliable Super-Z-type ferrule. The stripping guide is the clean, simple, and classic Mildrum that was popular on older Orvis cane rods. The ring hook keeper is installed in the cork handle just below the winding check in the style of Weir & Sons Rods of California.

Schroeder matches the nodes on his rods in a two-on-two pattern. In this configuration a node is matched to one other node with two clear splits (splines) of bamboo between them. The next set of two nodes up the rod is placed one spline over, creating a spiral of matched nodes separated by two clear splines up the length of the rod.

"I've talked to a lot of different people who have looked at a lot of different cane rods and almost all of them say it really doesn't make any difference where the nodes are placed as long as you've got some cane between them. I just like the two-on-two combination," Schroeder said.

Schroeder uses a milling machine that he designed himself to produce his rods.

"I designed it and had some of the parts made that I couldn't make myself. It's a good machine," he said.

Schroeder said that he runs the bamboo through the machine once to get it into a triangular shape and then he runs the strips through the milling machine a second time to get the taper in. Finally, he touches up any incongruities with a hand plane.

"My opinion is that the machine helps my accuracy. When I run the bamboo through the machine, I get a perfect triangle right off the bat. I'm not saying you can't do that with the hand plane, but each builder has his own methods. Using the machine helps me keep all the strips uniform. I don't have to worry about the side of one strip being a little different than the others. The strips will fit together perfectly," Schroeder said.

Schroeder flames the cane in all of his rods.

"I flame the bamboo to give it some tone and bring out the highlights. I'd say 90 percent of the rods I build are the darker tones. I don't get the cane really black—just a nice rich medium brown tone. I retain the golden node but keep the rest as uniformly brown as I can get it. I blue the ferrules to blend better with the tone of the flamed cane," he said.

Line guide wraps are transparent tan silk tipped with dark maroon. Ferrule ends have dark maroon wraps. Schroeder uses a polyurethane finish for all his rods.

"I think if polyurethane was available to Jim Payne he would have used it. Some builders think that the old varnishes were something special, but when Payne or Leonard or any of them ran out of varnish they went down to the local hardware store and bought another gallon. Just like we do. There was no sacred place to buy varnish. Back in 1940 there were probably only two or three companies making varnish in the country. It's what those rod builders did with the varnish when they got it. Was it the temperature they applied it at? How it was applied? A special brush? A way of putting the varnish on that no one else knew how to do? That's the real secret of varnish," he said.

Schroeder said that modern polyurethanes have ultraviolet light inhibitors, which he believes slows the inevitable aging and deterioration of the rod finish.

A final detail that Schroeder takes care of himself is the heavy-duty rod bag. There is a stiffening dole in it and an easy-to-grab looped tag for pulling the bag from the rod tube.

"I sew it myself. I wish I was a little better at sewing, but it gets the job done and I am getting better," he said.

It's one of the most functional rod bags I've seen.

When hard-pressed, Schroeder will say that he likes a nice, medium-fast action fly rod.

"I don't know any bamboo rod builder who really designs a rod taper anymore. All you need to do is look at all the rods that have been built in the last seventy-five years. In terms of tapers, somebody's been there, done that. What I do is take a taper and modify it a little here and a little there, that's about it," he said.

Schroeder said that his basic rod-building philosophy is that he simply tries to make the best rod that he can.

"You just can't have a bad day if you're a rod builder. It takes only one bad rod to lose twenty customers real quick," he said.

It's taken Don Schroeder a long time to get where he is today. He began building rods part-time in the late 1970s after he got home from full-time factory work.

"I spent twenty years working at some jobs I didn't like that much. I'd come home at night and build rods until I got tired, and then on Saturday and Sunday I'd build them all day long. Finally, I couldn't take it any longer. I went to full-time rod building in June of 1995. I'm doing what I want to do right now, and I earned it," Schroeder said.

Just like Don Schroeder's constant striving for excellence prohibits him from having a bad day building rods, his fine rods prohibit those who fish them from having a bad day on the stream.

January 2000. "I don't really change my rods too much," Don Schroeder said when I called the other day, "but what I do end up doing is occasionally making a limited edition or a special one-of-a-kind rod. I try to do that every year or every other year."

Schroeder made a commemorative rod to celebrate the 200th rod he built a few years back. He's close to 300 rods now.

"I've made close to 280 rods, but there are some I haven't counted. I did a limited edition bamboo Muskie rod for a company that is now out of business. That was too bad because they were one of the best plug companies I've ever seen. I live here in Wisconsin, and believe me, I've seen a lot and these guys were great," he said.

Schroeder said that his rod models have stayed basically the same, with two-piece and three-piece rods offered from 6 to 8½ feet. Line weights for the rods begin at a 3-weight for the 6-foot rods and increase incrementally to 6- or 7-weight for the 8½-foot models. He still makes four-sided rods but only on a special-order basis.

Most recently Schroeder has come out with a line of two-piece or three-piece salmon rods. They are available in 8½ foot, 7-weight; 8½ foot, 8-weight; 9 foot, 8-weight; and 9 foot, 9-weight.

"I don't sell a lot of them, but I have them there anyway. I actually just got done making one that's going to Canada, and I sent one out East a while ago," he said.

Schroeder is still partial to Payne tapers, but said that more than anything he tries to base his rods on a good medium to medium-fast action.

"They aren't slow rods, but they're not fast rods either, so I guess you could say that's kind of like a Payne. But I'll tell you, I could make every one of my rods with a Payne taper and they'd be great rods. If I had to pick three rodmakers who have influenced me the most, I'd say Payne, Dickerson, and Young. They made great fishing rods, and that's what I'm in business for. I don't build rods just to cast. My rods are made to fish, and to me there's a lot of difference. I don't care what kind of rod you got and how pretty it is—if it never gets fished, it's not a fishing rod," he said.

Schroeder said that he builds about forty rods a year but also does a lot of restoration work.

"I work on rods five days or sometimes six days a week. That's how I make my living. If I don't sell rods, I don't have any money, but if I don't make great rods, I'm out of business and I lose my reputation. So I want my rods to be the best I can build," he said.

Don Schroeder told me that he didn't foresee himself doing anything else other than building bamboo fly rods.

"I'm in it for the rest of my life," he said.

And that is good news for those of us who enjoy casting bamboo fly rods.

CHAPTER SIXTEEN

Jennifer Olsson Split-Cane Signature Rods by Carl-Johan Anderberg

February 2000. I'm on my way to a meeting with Gary Knighting on the high-tech end of town. Gary works for a company whose name is a jumble of letters that doesn't mean anything unless you're a computer nerd, but more importantly, he owns two of the first Jennifer Olsson Split-Cane Signature fly rods built by Swedish rodmaker Carl-Johan Anderberg. Gary has agreed to let me cast them over the lunch hour. We're meeting at Parking Lot CX03, which somehow sounds appropriate for a high-tech outfit. There is a big lawn there that is ideal for casting.

Gary is waiting for me with rod cases in hand when I arrive in my 1984 Oldsmobile Cierra. It's the oldest car in the high-tech parking lot. The first thing I notice are the rod cases. They are identical hard-bodied tubes covered with black Cordora nylon cloth. There is a nylon web handle and an adjustable nylon web shoulder strap. Near the zippered cap is an embroidered logo.

Carl-Johan Anderberg

PHOTO BY JARL ASKLUND

There is a split-cane rod in the middle of a green oval with Jennifer's name over the top of it. In the background there are embroidered green mountains. To the left some gorgeous red flowers bloom out of the oval. It's very nice. We head for the lawn with no further ado.

Gary tells me that the two rods were conceived to cover the majority of trouting waters that most anglers will encounter. The three-piece 7-foot 9-inch-long Midsummer is for a 4- or 5-weight fly line. The 4th of July, which is a three-piece 8-footer, is for a 5- or 6-weight fly line. Jennifer sews the colorful tie-dyed bags that protect the rods.

I choose to start with the 4th of July. The reel seat hardware consists of an aluminum cap with a down-sliding aluminum band over a flattened oiled wood spacer of what appears to be a burl wood. There is a thin aluminum cork check at the grip end of the spacer. The grip is western style, fashioned from thirteen rings of medium-grade cork. A ring-style hook keeper is wrapped in burgundy thread, which opens into three spiral wraps and then closes with three or four wraps.

The ferrules, which appear to be Bailey Woods SDs, all have similar burgundy wraps with the short open spiral on both the male and the female, as does the tip-top guide. The stripping guide appears slightly smaller in diameter than you would expect on an equivalent rod made by an American rodmaker. The cane is a pleasant golden brown with an ever so slightly swelled butt with three-on-three node spacing.

I rigged the rod with a Cortland 444 double-taper 6-weight line for the first series of casts. My initial impression upon casting was that the rod is snappy, but you still feel some bend into the butt, which is reminiscent of a Payne action. It seemed like a nice melding of deeper European rod actions that have been influenced by parabolic tapers with the quicker tipped American-style rod actions. It was a quite pleasant ride.

The rod cast effortlessly to 55 feet with a quick single haul and romped out to 75 feet with a half-hearted double haul. The power that reaches down into the butt of the rod becomes fully apparent on longer casts. The seemingly smaller-diameter stripping guide didn't impede shooting the fly line. After wanging away for distance for a few minutes, I concentrated my casts at actual fishing distances. The rod was responsive and easy to direct in the 15- to 40-foot range. The day was a bit breezy, and the rod had no difficulty cutting the line through the wind.

When I switched over to a 5-weight double-taper line, I noted that the rod speeded up a bit. It was also easier to control shock waves in the line on the false casts. Long distance casts were similar in length to the 6-weight, and the rod cast sweetly to my typical fishing distances. The 4th of July was one of a few rods I've cast where I could see applications for either the 5-weight or 6-weight line without losing the essence of the action that makes it fun to cast. I honestly could go with either line, depending on conditions.

The 4- or 5-weight Midsummer rod was appointed with the same hardware, wood spacer, grip, cork check, hook keeper, guide wrap color, and ferrule style as the 4th of July. I started off with the 5-weight double-taper line. The rod cast nicely close-in but seemed overlined at 60-foot and longer casts, although I could compensate by finessing the power stroke a bit. False casts tended to get shocky if my attention waned.

I switched over to the 4-weight double-taper line, and relief was instantaneous. The line cast smoothly to 60 feet with a single haul and shot nicely to 75 feet when double hauled. Very long distance casts required a modicum of attention to avoid overpowering the rod. I've found this to be the norm rather than the exception on many 4-weight bamboo fly rods I've cast. The rod shines at fishing distances to about 45 feet, where it is delicate and easy to direct. I would envision the Midsummer as a sweet date for mid-sized upland streams with a 4-weight line.

The origin of the Jennifer Olsson Split-Cane Signature rods is an interesting story. The root of Olsson's appreciation for bamboo is wonderfully recounted in her book, *Cast Again, Tales of a Fly-Fishing Guide* (The Lyons Press, 1996). An old fly fisher cajoles her into fishing the Pale Morning Dun hatch with his 7½-foot Payne on a Paradise Valley spring creek. If that didn't seal the deal on cane, the gift of a split-cane fly rod from her Swedish sweetheart and husband-to-be, Lars, at the Bozeman airport did. That fly rod just happened to have been made by Carl-Johan Anderberg.

"My husband-to-be at the time asked me what I wanted, and I said a split-cane fly rod. I thought I wanted it to be very light, so I asked for a 3-weight or a 4-weight for small streams. I didn't want a slow, slow action. I wanted a responsive action. Lars gave that information to Carl. What he came up with was a two-piece 7-foot 3-inch rod. I've really fished that rod a lot," Olsson said.

Olsson said that she got to thinking that it would be nice to have a longer rod with the same action for larger waters. She approached Anderberg about building the rod.

"Carl came up with a taper, and then I said that since I travel a lot I'd like it to be a three-piece rod. I didn't want a pet rod. I wanted a rod I could fish. I needed to be able to transport it easily," Olsson said.

Anderberg worked out the taper for a three-piece rod and came up with a 7-foot 9-inch, 4- or 5-weight rod.

"I fell in love with that rod. We christened it the Midsummer, and I fished it and fished it and fished it. After awhile I started thinking, What else do I want out of a rod? I thought it would be nice to have one that I could run a heavier line on because I usually fish with heavier lines, especially in the wind and on grayling waters. I wanted a little more punch. That's when Carl came up with the 4th of July, which is a 5- or 6-line weight rod," said Olsson.

Olsson said that once she had the pair of rods in hand, it occurred to her that between the two they would cover just about any kind of trout and grayling experience that she would want to have.

"Eventually it occurred to me that because of my interest in fly-fishing, people approach me and ask what kind of fly rod I'd recommend. At first I'd suggest various graphite rods, and then I thought that I'm really fishing split cane most of the time. I thought, Why not recommend the rods I fish every day. That's when I approached Carl, whose work I really like, and suggested we make an effort together. That's how I started marketing the two rods. It's been more than a year now," Olsson said.

Olsson said that the Midsummer and 4th of July rods have evolved somewhat from the earlier models I cast.

"I thought I wanted to shrink the hardware a bit, so we are going to a truncated ferrule. We've also changed the hardware on the reel seat from aluminum to nickel silver, but the taper design is the same," she said.

Olsson said that the two rods will be marketed as models, which means that the burgundy wraps, grip, and reel seat hardware will be standardized in all but very special cases.

"This rod would be perfect for someone getting into cane who may not be up on all the terminology, details, and options available on a cane rod. Having a specific model rod solves that. You know what color the wraps are going to be and how the rod is going to look," she said.

Olsson said that she's very respectful of Anderberg's attention to detail when he builds a fly rod and that they have a very good relationship.

"I like everything about the rods. I fish hard and I don't want a piece of equipment that requires more of me than I require of it. I'm really interested in the action, but on the other hand, I wouldn't want an ugly rod, either. Cosmetics are important, too. I meet a lot of people with cane anxiety. They don't feel comfortable with a cane rod as a fishing tool. It's almost like they don't want to touch it. I use my fly rods. I've had these rods in boats and on horseback, and I've caught some very large brown trout with them. I really enjoy the heck out of them," she said.

As luck would have it, Carl Anderberg speaks English a lot better than I speak Swedish. I learned through e-mail correspondence that Anderberg started making bamboo fly rods in 1972. Anderberg is a schoolteacher in Sweden but estimates he's made 200 to 250 rods on a part-time basis. It was only a matter of time before

I decided I'd better talk with him on the telephone. I was curious to learn if he thought there were differences between American-made split-cane rods and European split-cane rods.

"It's hard to explain the difference between action in European and American rods, but I think we favor slower tapers here. We like a little more punch. We use so many different types of actions here. I think Americans are more limited in that," Anderberg said.

Anderberg, like many European anglers I've corresponded with, said he personally prefers the fuller parabolic action of the Ritz rods in an 8-foot length. It's always surprising to me that Americans never really embraced parabolics, although Paul Young made some excellent designs, as did Jim Payne. It's not likely to change, either. Many fly fishers switching from graphite to cane rods look for tippy, quick rod actions rather than the more full, complex action of a parabolic design.

Anderberg said that he builds only custom rods to a fly fisher's specifications.

"I prefer to see the customer cast before I build a rod for them, but that wasn't the case for Mrs. Olsson. I knew her husband, Lars, and we discussed the type of action that she liked, which I would call an American action, and that's how I came up with the rod that turned out to be her wedding present. It's the one she wrote about in her book. She obviously liked the rod, so we had a starting point for the later rods," he said.

Anderberg said that the difficulty he had when making the Midsummer and the 4th of July was that Olsson wanted the rods to cast the same as the two-piece 7-foot 3-inch "wedding rod," but she wanted them to be longer and of a three-piece design.

"I wasn't sure that I could transfer the action from the shorter, two-piece rod to the longer, three-piece rod. As you know, ferrules interfere heavily on any action, and it was especially true on this design. I solved the problem by using a convex taper for the midsection and in many ways had to reconstruct the rod entirely," he said.

Anderberg said he characterizes the actions of both rods as an "American three-quarter action." He uses three-on-three node spacing on all the rods he makes. Perfection stripping guides, line guides, and tip-tops are used on current models. The wood insert in the reel seat is a nicely figured Swedish wood known as Masur bjork. It's a birch, also known as sallow birch or sallow burl.

"Originally I used an oil finish on the insert, but I've switched to a varnish now, and as you know, we are now using nickel silver fittings," he said.

Anderberg uses a polyurethane finish on the cane.

"I developed a special way of applying the finish that I'm quite secretive about. The polyurethane is tricky to use, and you have to have certain methods," he said.

The finish on the rods is very fine. Anderberg commented that although his shop may get a bit dusty, he walks very slowly and carefully in it when he is applying the finish to a rod.

As is the case with most rodmakers, Anderberg says that good cork is difficult to come by.

"Cork for the grip is a scarce item because the champagne industry in France buys it up. I buy as much ordinary cork as I can. It works well enough and isn't too expensive. You shouldn't have to pay a dollar for a ring of cork. It should really go for a few cents," he said.

Anderberg came to rod making, like many makers, through his enjoyment of fly fishing, but his evolution as a maker from that point is considerably different from many Amercian makers.

"I'm self-taught. When I first came across some bamboo culms, I couldn't even split them. I ruined two or three stalks just trying to split them; then I came across a little book written in the 1950s from a Danish author. What I got from that book was the understanding that a cane rod should have six strips. Everything else I learned on my own. I got tapers by measuring rods that I've come across," he said.

Anderberg said that it took ten years before he thought his rods were good enough to be made for other anglers.

"Cane rod building became very popular here when the Garrison book came out in 1980. There were plenty of builders here and they were all Garrsion fans, but by then I had developed my own methods and didn't see any reason to get involved," he said.

Anderberg planed his first rods in wooden blocks and then went to a beveller of his own design and construction.

"I used the beveller for six or eight years, but then I went to hand planing the rods with metal planing forms. It's simpler for me, since I don't make production rods. You don't save as much time as people think when you use a machine," he said.

Anderberg states emphatically, and to my way of thinking, refreshingly, that he is not a professional.

"I'm not a professional in any way. I build rods for the fun of it. I like building rods for people because I want to please them. That's why I do it. It's a good reason for me and for the people I build the rods for. Right now I'll probably just build the Olsson rods this year. Maybe six to ten rods. I don't want to force it. I want to keep things good," he said.

As much as anything, the Jennifer Olsson Signature rods represent a pleasant mixing of European rod design ideas with American ideas. They are a European's take on what an American fly rod action is all about. When you cast the 4th of July there is just a whisper of the deeper action that Anderberg says is more common in European rods. You feel it almost subliminally right above the cork. The rods are made for casting line more than shooting line.

Jennifer Olsson said, "The rods fit my whole take on fly fishing anymore—what I like to get out of the sport. It means a lot to me after teaching casting and guiding for so long."

The Signature rods are a fine partnership between Europe and America and would fish nicely on any continent.

March 2001. Jennifer Olsson told me that she is adding a new rod to complement the 4th of July and Midsummer models.

"The new model is called the Castilleja. It's a three-piece 8-footer for a 5- or 6-weight line with a parabolic action. This rod will appeal to those who want a snappier response to lifting when fishing weighted nymphs and a faster casting action overall. It's flamed darker than its sisters. The ferrules and hardware are the same as the others, but the wood spacer is darker. It's delightfully smooth and quick," Olsson said.

Olsson said that her husband, Lars, and she continue to be smitten with rod actions and designs. They're busy talking with other Scandinavian rodmakers in hopes of introducing their work to American bamboo aficionados.

CHAPTER SEVENTEEN

In the Bamboo Forest

ANDY ROYER, GLENN BRACKETT, JANA RUSH, AND I ARE standing outside the airport at Guangzhou (formerly known as Canton) in the early morning. We've just finished a fifteen-hour airplane ride in a China Southern Boeing 777 that involved a few hours of rough air over the Aleutians and several weird Chinese movies that didn't include subtitles.

The very early morning light, high humidity, smog, and jet lag have conspired to make my first impression of China appear to be in black and white. There is a small park just across the way where a cadre of older Chinese citizens are serenely doing tai chi. They float through the air like so many ghosts. There are other citizens volleying a badminton birdie back and forth. A few joggers slowly, rhythmically circle the park. I am relieved that one of the women doing tai chi has chosen to wear a red scarf this morning. It proves that China does indeed come in color.

We have come to southeastern China to see for ourselves where the Tonkin cane used to make the finest split-cane fly rods grows. None of this would have been possible without the help of Andy Royer, who has been importing Tonkin cane for rodmakers since 1995.

"I got into bamboo with a high school friend in 1994. He'd seen bamboo flooring being made in a factory in China, and we decided to get into the flooring business," Royer explained to me on the long flight to China.

Royer said that his interest in bamboo flooring came from ecological concerns over the use of hardwoods.

"Our goal was to introduce bamboo as a substitute for hardwood in the developed countries. We figured that flooring was a good place to start. Unlike hardwoods, bamboo, which is a grass, matures every three to four years. If you look at five acres of mature bamboo versus five acres of hardwood, you can harvest and use fully one-third of that bamboo per year. There's no way that's going to happen with hardwood," Royer said.

Royer said that bamboo has been used in undeveloped countries "forever." It's often referred to as the "poor man's timber" because of its strength, weight, and usefulness.

"While we were doing the flooring, we started importing Tonkin cane for agricultural use to help subsidize our business. Eventually, we began to sell some to rodmakers. Did you know that Westerners first became aware of Tonkin when it was used as poles to carry rugs from the Orient? It was used because of its great strength," Royer said.

Royer eventually met Daryll Whitehead, an Oregon rodmaker, who was trying to find a source of quality rod-making bamboo. Whitehead hadn't been able to find a supplier who could provide him with the straw-colored bamboo coveted by rodmakers that was unmarred by slash marks or burn marks made by growers to identify their bamboo.

Whitehead and rodmaker George Maurer ultimately put up the cash to buy 3,000 poles through a Hong Kong supplier. Although it took ten months to put the shipment together, it was unacceptable when it arrived. The cane was green and had slash marks and burn marks.

"Around that time Daryll gave me a chapter from a book on how to select bamboo for rod builders. That's when I began to understand there was a real market among rodmakers for Tonkin cane and I began to concentrate on importing it. In 1997 I found a few sources and decided that I would go over to China and select the bamboo myself. The key is that every piece must be inspected," Royer said.

One of those sources was Cai Shao Tu, the vice director of the Bamboo Products Factory in Aozai, a small town in Huaiji County.

"One of the more difficult things I had to do was to explain that I wanted the straw-colored bamboo. The Chinese consider this to be a less healthy culm of bamboo than one that has a little green in it. I also needed larger poles unmarred by the burn or slash marks that growers make on the bamboo to identify it. These were very unusual requests. Cai worked very hard to meet my needs for the size of bamboo necessary to build rods and the right looks," Royer said.

It is Cai who meets us at the airport, along with a hired van and entourage of helpers, including a young translator named Shelly from Yangshuo. Everything in China is a group project— even picking up a few Tonkin cane pilgrims at the airport.

After a remarkable full-course early morning meal in a nearby uptown hotel, we pile into the van and begin the four-hour drive to the hamlet of Aozai, which is located northwest of Guangzhou in the heart of bamboo country in the Sui River drainage.

The drive out of Guangzhou, whose population I estimate conservatively to be about the size of Los Angeles, is memorable.

There are almost no stoplights, and the streets are a confusion of cars, vans, bicycles, motorcycles, and pedestrians. The motion is constant, as is the sound of honking horns. It soon becomes apparent that there is a Tao of sorts at work in all of this. The trick is to never stop moving. If another vehicle honks, you move slightly out of the way whether you are a pedestrian or on a bicycle or motorcycle. You gracefully glance off your fellow citizens. Stopping to look both ways before you enter or cross an intersection, like is done in the West, would be the kiss of death. It would bring the slow snaking motion of the entire city to a halt, and the odds are that it would never get started again.

As we move slowly through the city, Glenn, who has made bamboo fly rods for the Winston Rod Company for years, notes how bamboo is used to prop up porches, build scaffold, hold up tarps, carry trade goods, and even form the cages that chickens are carried in to the market.

"Look at all the bamboo—it's the two-by-four of China!" he exclaims.

Eventually we ooze our way out of the city. That doesn't mean that there aren't still pedestrians on the road, because China is a nation of walkers; or that there aren't motorcycles, which are the primary motorized transport in the country; or that there is a dearth of bicycles, which are the transport of the masses—it just means that there is not a solid-moving snaking mass of them.

In the countryside every backyard is home to chickens, every pond is home to ducks, every bit of soil is growing food. And on every corner there is a market. Almost all the food consumed is grown locally. That means the chicken you eat tonight most likely was the one walking around the backyard earlier or the one you saw stuffed in the bamboo basket on the back of a bicycle.

Overall the drive to Aozai is on the conservative side of harrowing—at least if you are a Westerner. It's just another day in the life of China for everyone else. None of the close calls on the highway are close enough to even elicit a sigh from the driver. And the law of the land is the Teflon Tao, where everything bounces, slides, or glances off everything else.

In Aozai there is one main road through town, where the ubiquitous market, motorcycle repair shop, hardware store, fabric shop, and restaurant reside—and pretty much any other shop you might need to survive in a small town.

The residents can't get enough of us. The most common expression is one of glee. Children walk up, look at us, and just fall into big belly laughs. They all want to practice their English on us. Everywhere we go we hear little voices intoning "Hello, hello, hello" in surprisingly understandable accents. Of course, that's about the only English they speak, but it is a proud hello. Jana is a special attraction. There is a good chance that she is the first Western woman any of them have ever seen.

Cai takes us to the local restaurant for a less formal meal than the one we consumed in Guangzhou. We are served only fish, shrimp, beef (?), bamboo shoots, little mollusks in a soup, fiddlehead ferns, and chicken that has been summarily chopped into chopstick-manageable pieces replete with bones. Nothing is wasted. The entrance to the restaurant is a biology teacher's delight of aquariums filled with carplike fish, eels, mussels, and snakes—all alive and at your service for dinner.

After lunch Cai takes us to the bamboo factory. All varieties of bamboo are brought here via the river whose shore adjoins the factory, or over the highway from the nearby forests. A key to understanding China is to understand that bamboo is everything—you eat it; you make scaffolds with it; you make furniture, shades, screens, curtains, and beanpoles with it. In terms of weight, strength, its renewable nature, and usefulness, it outstrips wood and even steel in many ways.

The Tonkin cane that Andy is interested in is painstakingly cleaned of lichens, molds, and dirt by factory workers (usually women) who rub it by hand with sand and then rinse it in either long concrete tanks or the river. It is then stacked pole by pole into a teepee shape to dry and season to the desirable straw color. Once dried and seasoned, it is stored under the cover of a roof until Andy is able to sort through it.

"I typically have to look at 10,000 culms to get 6,000 culms for import," Andy says as he looks down a 12-foot culm to ascertain its straightness.

The bamboo that Royer sells to rodmakers is 2 inches or more in diameter and 12 feet long. It's sold in ten-pole bundles.

"I use two classifications for the culms. A 'B pole' is a pole that I think a rod builder can not easily use to make into a first-class fly rod. Either it's too lightweight, has too many curves or kinks, is too green, is too full of bug marks or other incapacitating marks, or is just too ugly to make a high quality fly rod with," Royer said.

Royer sells B poles to nurseries for use in gardening and craft projects and as fencing material. It also is occasionally sold to rod builders for experimental or educational purposes.

"If the B pole isn't too lightweight, you can still make a rod from it, but it's harder to work with. I've been to some rod-making gatherings where there are hundreds of cane rods. You see a wide range of quality in the cane that has been used. Some of the rods have marks and imperfections in the cane. They cast just fine, but if you're after the kind of aesthetic that today's builder aspires to, they just don't get it," Royer said.

Royer selects "A poles" specifically for rod making.

"The first thing I do is make an immediate judgment about the aesthetics of the culm—it's either good, bad, or worse than bad. A bad pole can still become an A pole if it's very straight and heavy and not marked up by bugs. A worse-than-bad-pole doesn't have a chance. I hold every pole before I buy it. I pick it up and check the weight, straightness, surface clarity, and overall appearance," Royer said.

Royer said that it's important to note that the Chinese have already sorted the poles before he even looks at them and eliminated most with slash or burn marks. They also sort out grossly crooked or curved poles.

"Over time the Chinese have gotten much better at supplying the kind of bamboo I want. They know which of the farmers in the area have rod-making quality bamboo and that's what they buy for me to look at," Royer said.

Unlike some Tonkin cane importers, Royer does not straighten the poles.

"The straightening process involves heating up the bamboo to the point of scorching it and then putting that hot section in a fulcrum and stressing it to make it straight. That causes an unnatural modification of the power fibers. Sometimes the heat isn't severe enough to scorch the surface. The problem is that a pole may not have the appearance of having been heat straightened, but when the rodmaker starts working with the strips they behave differently than strips in other parts of the pole because they have been stressed," Royer said.

The routine for the next few days is predictable. Andy heads down to the factory and sorts bamboo. Glenn assists. I take photographs, and Jana paints watercolors, much to the delight of the children who accompany their parents to work at the factory.

Andy is workmanlike in his devotion to the goal of selecting enough poles to put a decent shipment together. The likelihood of that goal is initially jeopardized because a number of the culms have been water damaged by the unusually wet spring. Eventually Cai finds additional poles for Andy to look at.

Glenn, the bamboo rodmaker, is a little less workmanlike. He has a dreamy look on his face. The only explanation is that here you have a man who has worked with Tonkin cane much of his adult life and now finds himself surrounded by it. There is a delightful twinkle in his eye.

Once in awhile Andy or Glenn holds up an especially good culm for the other to examine and then ooh and ahh over. A typical A pole weighs in at 6 pounds. Andy and Glenn are dumbfounded when they come across two high-quality heavyweight poles that weigh 11 pounds apiece.

"A lot of power fibers here," Glenn exclaims.

The work at the factory is punctuated by delicious meals at Cai's home on the northern end of town. Breakfast is usually some sort of noodles purchased from a vender next door along with a doughy roll with pork inside. Dinner, which is prepared by Cai's wife, whom we call "Mrs. Cai," typically features shrimp, chicken, fiddlehead ferns, parsnips, sweet peppers, bamboo shoots, hot peppers, and fish. It's all cooked fresh in a wok over a hot fire fueled with dried bamboo. The eating is exquisite.

One evening after dinner Cai shows us a rod blank he has made himself using a planing form that George Maurer gave him when he visited the bamboo factory two years ago. The work is amazingly good for an apprentice rodmaker. He also has a finished rod—he made the blank and sent it to George in Pennsylvania for varnish and hardware. It's a fine-looking instrument. Cai gently grills Glenn through Shelly, the translator, about getting hardware so he can make finished rods by himself.

In a final flourish Cai breaks out a tool he has designed and had machined for roughing out the triangular splines for rods. It's basically two wheels. One acts as a guide and the other is a cutter. They mesh together to make the initial cuts. The bamboo is pushed through the cutters or possibly they are attached to a machine. In any event, Glenn says, "I've never seen anything like it. It's revolutionary."

We finish the evening off by tossing a Frisbee back and forth among Glenn, Andy, myself, and Cai's son, Jackie, in front of the house. The endeavor draws a crowd of onlookers.

On another evening the foreign trade representative for the county takes us all to dinner. Serious toasting with rice wine and beer is the order of the day. The Chinese have an endearing habit of filling your wine glass to the brim every time you take a sip. You learn to not drink quickly if you plan to walk home that evening.

The dinner is sumptuous. The twelve courses include fish, snails, shrimp, chicken, fish heads, fried rice, bamboo shoots, eggs, ferns, peppers, peanuts that are eaten one at a time with chopsticks, sweet sticky buns, and a curious item that the Chinese call "fox." Needless to say it is dog, and the hometown boys get a great laugh when we taste it. They know full well where we have come from.

Along with an understanding of bamboo, you must also understand the motorcycle if you are to understand China. Motorcycles are everywhere. All of them appear to be about 125-cc machines. Although there are different brand names emblazoned on the gas tanks, all of the bikes are exactly the same. The Chinese have made an art form of piling people on to motorcycles. It is not uncommon to see a family of four or five—mom, dad, and three youngsters—happily buzzing down the road. In the smaller towns, having a motorcycle is a sign that you have arrived; few Chinese have cars here. The majority of people ride bicycles or walk.

Although riding a motorcycle is as natural to the Chinese as walking, it isn't for me. I haven't ridden a motorcycle for over thirty years, but I still have the scars from the last time I did. The problem is that I will have to ride if I want to get up into the forest where the Tonkin cane grows. And I would not miss that for the world.

Cai has arranged for enough motorcycles for our little group. The pairings work out to Cai, Jackie, and Glenn; Andy and Shelly; and Jana and me. My very brief reacquaintance with the subtitles of the world of motorcycles consists of a quick run down to the outskirts of Aozai. I shift nicely up through the gears, but my masterful downshift from fourth to first leaves a patch of rubber on the road. I hear small children laughing when they hear the screeching rubber. I am too petrified with fear to look at them. Upon arrival at the house I declare that I'm A-OK to go. All I have to do is cruise down the main highway, take off on a dirt road, get the motorbike on to a little ferry, cross a river, and motor up a dirt road to the forest. "Piece of cake," I tell the group. Cai has a worried look on his face. Jana doesn't look too well either, but she smiles bravely.

Things go better than expected on the highway. A big wedding ceremony on the path to the ferry proves challenging, if only because everyone believes that I know what I'm doing. I just hope they've got their Teflon Tao shield going and manage to slide out of the way.

The trip actually goes surprisingly well. We navigate our way on and off the ferry without incident. With the exception of a very narrow bridge, the ride up the dirt road to the bamboo forest goes smoothly. I take time to enjoy the scenery every now and then. Jana even releases her death grip on my ribs once in awhile. I finally make a successful downshift from fourth to third gear. I am beginning to feel like a full-fledged member of the Tonkin Angels Motorcycle Club.

We wind our way along the river for a ways and then ascend up into the mountains, passing rice paddies along the way. The road ultimately leads to a small logging village. There is an archway with Chinese characters on it across the road. Eight-foot sections of a cedarlike log are neatly decked along the road. There are terraced rice paddies along the small drainage just outside the village. The steep hillsides surrounding us are thick in Tonkin cane. Its bluish sheen is unmistakable. It is gorgeous.

Before we can do anything, we must sit down with the head honcho of the village for tea. Nothing happens in China without a cup of tea first. It doesn't matter that it's about eighty degrees outside. I notice the village women hoisting their little children up on to the motorcycle seats as we sip the bitter tea. When Jana turns to take a photograph, they scatter like a covey of quail.

The trail up into the forest is a mosaic of light and shadow. Songbirds are flitting back and forth from the Tonkin to broad-leafed banana trees. They are the first birds I've seen in China. There is about a thirty-acre clear-cut across the valley where the Tonkin has been harvested. The Tonkin regenerates on its own by suckering, very much like the aspen does in the Rocky Mountains. The grove will fully mature in ten years. Good-quality poles for rod making can be harvested three to four years after that.

As we wander up the trail, Shelly translates for one of the forest workers. He says that the Tonkin grows in all diameters. An interesting point is that when the shoot first pushes up out of the soil it is the diameter that it will be when mature. Most of the culms we see are in the 1-inch-or-so diameter range, but on occasion we see a 2-inch or larger diameter stem that would be appropriate for rod making. Cai is busy cutting fresh Tonkin shoots for dinner. He recommends that we taste the shoots raw. They are quite good.

The Tonkin is extremely quick growing. A shoot can grow as much as a foot a day. The bamboo will grow to full size and diameter in four months, but most of that growth is water. The culm becomes more dense over time.

There is a fan of leaves that come out from one side of a node. The side that the leaves are on, the next node up, alternates 180 degrees to the other side. The space between the nodes is smooth and greenish blue. It's gorgeous stuff.

Eventually the trail peters out, and we return to the village. Cai wraps the Tonkin shoots in newspaper, and we mount up for the ride back to Aozai. Other than one little bitty curve I miss, where we make a slow-motion crash into a muddy hillside, the trip home is uneventful. Cai thinks the mishap is one of the funniest things he has seen in a long time. He laughs so hard he almost falls on the ground.

Later on, dinner is a bean dish flavored with a beef bone and carrots. The Tonkin shoots are served on the side. Cai lifts some Tonkin shoots to his mouth with his bamboo chopsticks and speaks the first English I've heard him say the whole trip.

"A pole!" he exclaims and then laughs like a child.

Dessert is a delicacy called sticky rice. It's very time consuming and difficult to make. A ball of rice is slow cooked in bamboo leaves. The inside of the rice is filled with nuts, fruits, and goodies. It's absolutely delicious. Afterwards we clean our teeth with bamboo toothpicks.

Bamboo is indeed life here.

The next morning we pack for the trip home. As crazy as I am about bamboo fly rods and as happy as I was to see where this beautiful grass grows, the most difficult thing I have to do in China is say good-bye to Cai, his wife, Jackie, his wife's family, and Shelly. They have treated us like family. There has been an unexplainable grace in the way they have taken care of us.

After the mandatory group photographs, smiles, and handshakes, the hired van comes to take us back to the airport in Guangzhou. At the last moment Mrs. Cai presents each of us with a little care package of sticky rice for the journey.

It's still wrapped in bamboo leaves.

CHAPTER EIGHTEEN

Beginner's Cane

May 1996. Several years ago I was at a dinner party and struck up a conversation with another fly fisher. When I mentioned in passing that I enjoyed fishing bamboo fly rods, he looked at me as if I were some sort of cult member. And I can understand why. There is a certain mystery to fishing bamboo fly rods, especially for those new to bamboo, that is both seductive and frustrating.

I didn't know anything about cane rods twenty-five years ago when I started buying them at garage sales in Colorado. It didn't take long to learn that unlike graphite or fiberglass fly rods, there can be very wide variations in the quality of bamboo rods. The garage sale rods I bought were euphemistically referred to as wet fly action, which simply meant that the action was so far into the handle of the rod that you could barely cast them. Most of those rods went for $5 to $20 and were of uniformly poor quality.

As I got more interested in bamboo, I began to find fly shops that handled better quality split-cane rods on consignment. I made a point to always cast all the rods and note the ones that I liked. I also began to meet people who could explain to me what to look for in a quality split-cane fly rod. And finally, I became acquainted with custom cane rod builders, such as Mike Clark and Homer Jennings, who had made a study of casting and analyzing as many makes and models of cane rods as they could get their hands on.

I'll admit that my initial experience with bamboo fly rods was a little uneven. I bought some poor quality rods, but I learned about bamboo in the process and that was half the fun. I often stripped, refinished, and referruled my garage sale rods just for practice.

Interest in bamboo fly rods has steadily grown with the increased popularity of fly-fishing in general. There are now more custom cane rod builders working in the United States than there have been in the past several decades.

More and more fly fishers are curious about bamboo's reputation for beauty, casting sensitivity, and control, but many believe that the cost of a quality split-cane rod is beyond their reach. That may be true. New custom-built rods run anywhere from $900 to $1,200 on the average, but perfectly serviceable previously owned cane fly rods are still available for the cost of a premium graphite fly rod ($400 to $600).

There are several ways for anglers new to bamboo to find a rod. The key is to talk with people who have some experience with split-cane rods. You'll find that certain rod names, such as Granger, Phillipson, and Heddon, consistently come up when quality rods at reasonable prices are mentioned. These American-made rods are commonly referred to as production rods. They were mass produced roughly from the 1920s through the 1960s. The makers of these rods were able to achieve a surprisingly consistent level of performance when producing the rods even though they were made in relatively large numbers.

Most of the production rod companies offered a number of models of fly rods. The cane used for all the rods was good, but the choicest material was often reserved for the premium models. Hardware and guide wraps were top-of-the-line on premium models. These premium models command premium prices today, but lower and midlevel models are affordable and still capable of offering many years of fly-fishing pleasure.

The key to judging the quality of any fly rod is to cast it. If you like the way a cane rod casts, that's important. The more rods you can cast, the more able you'll be to judge what you like in a cane rod. But there can be pitfalls when it comes to purchasing cane.

"When it comes to judging a cane rod, I can throw a lot of mechanics at you like determining whether ferrules are made from aluminum or nickel silver or how to determine if the rod is delaminating or the tip has a set, but that's just going to frustrate and confuse many beginners," said Mike Clark, the master custom rod builder, rod dealer, and owner of South Creek, Ltd., in Lyons, Colorado.

Clark suggested that those wanting to learn about split-cane fly rods should start by getting hold of the catalogs of major rod dealers such as Martin Keane, Bob Corsetti, and Len Codella. These catalogs often list upwards of a hundred previously owned bamboo fly rods along with some new custom-built rods. The catalogs list a broad range of rod makes and models and evaluate their condition. More importantly, you can call the dealers, explain your needs to them, and ask their advice. Most allow you to return any rod you're not happy with within a three- to five-day inspection period. Typically, very few rods are returned because both the dealer and the buyer are able to discuss the rod over the telephone.

"There are always exceptions, but I'd recommend you stay away from the Montagues, Horrocks-Ibbotsons, and some of the South Bends. I'd also stay away from any Japanese bamboo rod or a rod without a name on it. Along with the Grangers, Phillipsons, and Heddons, the Orvis impregnated rods can be a good buy for beginners. But always cast the rods. If it feels good, that will go a long way in helping you make your decision," Clark said.

Martin Keane, whose catalog, *Classic Rods & Tackle, Inc.*, first appeared twenty-seven years ago and is the oldest catalog of split-cane rods, added these ideas for those new to cane.

"The best present market for rods in the $400 to $500 range is Granger, Heddon, Phillipson, Orvis Madison, single-tip rods and some English rods that are quite excellent," Keane said.

Keane said bamboo fly rods longer than 8 feet often decline in value because they aren't as likely to be the kind of rods you want to fish all the time.

"These become a more specialized rod—maybe for large flies in western rivers, nymph rods, streamer rods, bass bugging rods. They're the rods you probably won't use all the time. A person may spend $500 to $1,000 for a rod they'll use quite a bit, but when it comes to a specialized rod, they tend to want to spend less. There also seems to be an inverse-type formula where there are a lot more big rods than there are little rods," Keane said.

Although a bit heavier, these longer rods in 8½- and 9-foot lengths can offer an opportunity for beginning cane enthusiasts to own a rod at a very reasonable price.

"You can also surely get into a decent, serviceable 8-foot cane rod for a 5- or 6-weight line for $500. We sell hundreds of them every year, and they are wonderful. These are your Grangers, Heddons, and Phillipsons. They made fine rods. The more reasonable prices for these particular rods have a lot to do with the fact that so many were produced. If Bill Phillipson had produced only 1,200 to 1,400 rods, like many of the custom builders, they'd cost a lot more than they do. It just has to do with scarcity. The fact that so many were made is to the benefit of someone looking for a good but not terribly expensive cane rod," Keane said.

Keane, like Clark, strongly recommends that those new to cane cast the rods.

"I have people call all the time asking if a rod their neighbor is trying to sell them is worth the price. I always ask them if they've cast it and like it. The price is what it costs you to own the rod. It's not necessarily what it's worth. You can spend a large sum of money on a rod that might not be suitable to your personality or casting style or how you want to use it. In that case, you don't need it no matter what the price is," Keane said.

Bob Corsetti, whose *Rods & Reels* catalog comes out of New Hampshire, suggests that graphite fly rod casters new to cane modify their casting style a bit before they test cast a cane rod.

"I tell them to get their elbow back down near their side and to just relax. I want them to cast the rod and forget about shooting a lot of line. Many graphite rod casting styles are for shooting line, and that may not apply completely to casting a cane rod. I also suggest using double-taper lines that are more flexible, without the hard, slippery finish used in lines designed to shoot," Corsetti said.

Corsetti works as much as possible with beginning cane rod casters.

"I can usually start people in the $400 range. I get calls now and then where someone says he wants to start using a cane rod and do I have anything for $200. I usually have to say there's nothing you'd want to fish with in that range," Corsetti said.

Options for beginning cane rod casters other than working through the catalogs include visiting specialty fly shops that sell cane rods or have previously owned cane rods on consignment. Some cane rod builders also deal in previously owned rods. The values assigned to various rod models in the catalogs can be used as a rough measure for pricing rods found in shops, but potential buyers should note that some catalog prices may be higher than "on the street" values because the catalog dealers usually inspect and evaluate the rods they sell and are more likely to stand behind them.

Another possibility is a single-tip cane rod or a "not-in-original-condition" rod. Most cane rods come with two tips; it's a kind of insurance policy against a broken tip ruining your day of fishing. Rotating usage between the two tips also extends the life of the tips, but a beginner who is anxious to get the feel of a cane rod can often buy a single-tip rod that will provide years of service for several hundred dollars less. If the single tip breaks, a replacement can be made.

Some custom builders offer excellent new one-tip rods at substantial savings. Mike Clark builds the St. Vrain Special, a one-tip rod that uses Phillipson Peerless impregnated blanks that were the finest blanks Phillipson made. The rods have wood spacers on the reel seat, Leonard Super Swiss ferrules, and all nickel silver hardware. They sell for between $400 and $500.

Cane rods that are not in original condition can also provide excellent fishing tools for those who want to get the feel of quality cane at reasonable prices. These "not original" rods have often been refinished, have a tip missing or a shortened tip, lack the original rod bag or tube, or have some other flaw that make them less appealing to collectors or more fanatical bamboo enthusiasts—but they often cast and fish just as well as the original. They can be great buys.

Finally, some English cane rods, such as Partridge, Sharps, and Hardy, may have somewhat different actions and tapers than American-built cane rods, but they can be quite sweet and reasonably priced.

The trick to getting into cane, like anything else, is to educate yourself. Talk to other cane enthusiasts, get hold of the catalogs, read, and, most important, cast as many cane rods as you can get your hands on. Find out what you like in a cane rod.

Martin Keene said that the learning process with cane rods is the spice of the whole experience. Most of us who are hooked on cane wouldn't have it any other way. The more you learn, the more you want to know.

Eventually, as you get into cane, you may be fortunate enough to find yourself casting a top-quality example of a rod built by one of the great masters—a Payne, a Garrison, a Dickerson. It may be that you can't buy it, but you've finagled your chance from a friend or acquaintance to take the rod for a spin. When you first cast it, you feel the great care and skill that the rod builder put into it. It comes through in the casting of the rod. You know it's one of a kind. And you know that the builder was proud of it. His name is right there on the rod. It means that he built that rod and if anything goes wrong you know where to find him.

None of that comes with a graphite rod, and it makes it worth your time to figure out cane. Believe me. And besides, cane is just plain fun to cast.

Yes, it's a cult. But it's a wonderful cult.

February 2000. Interest in everything about bamboo fly rods has increased dramatically over the past five years. More hobbyists are making their own split-cane rods than at any time in the last fifty years. The number of professional bamboo rodmakers has skyrocketed, although it's important to note that many of those rodmakers work part-time at the craft. The number of full-time rodmakers who derive the majority of their livelihood from the handcrafting and sale of split-cane rods still remains small.

The heightened interest in cane has resulted in a scarcity of vintage bamboo fly rods and an increase in the asking price for the rods that are still available. An 8-foot Granger, Heddon, or Phillipson rod in good to excellent condition that might have gone for $400 to $500 in 1995 can fetch from $600 to $800 in 2000. Buyers of vintage cane rods need to be on their toes more than ever in the present market. A name-brand "bargain" cane rod can be seriously flawed. Look for short tips, sets, loose ferrules, nonoriginal reproduced sections, lifts in the bamboo, and breakage that is repaired with "invisible" wraps. Expect values on 8-foot and shorter rods to be high. Some good deals for quality fishable rods in $8\frac{1}{2}$- and 9-foot lengths are still available.

The actual marketplace for vintage cane rods has also shifted from an almost exclusive catalog and consignment base five years ago to one that relies heavily on the Internet. Buyers new to cane should beware of Internet purchases, at least in the beginning. Catalog dealers still offer advice and personal treatment to prospective buyers and typically a 3- to 5-day return privilege. A sight-unseen purchase over the Internet with no return privilege can be risky to anyone—let alone first-time buyers. It may cost a little more to purchase a rod through a dealer, but you're paying for some insurance, and that isn't a bad idea even for experienced bamboo rod collectors.

The increasing prices and scarcity in the vintage rod market have turned a number of newcomers to bamboo rods built by contemporary rodmakers. The price for a new split-cane rod from an established full-time rodmaker has probably increased about $500 in the past five years to an average cost of $1,500 to $1,600. One of the things that you typically get when buying from a reputable dealer is lifetime service. You should have confidence that the rodmaker will be around in the future if your rod needs repair. Perfectly serviceable rods from somewhat less-known rodmakers can go anywhere from $1,100 to $1,500 and often come with the same commitment that the long-established rod builders make. Once again, the key to value is to cast the rods. Get a rod you like casting and want to fish with.

One bright spot for newcomers to cane is an increase in the availability of what I call starter cane rods. These are typically single-tip two-piece rods that are produced by established rodmakers. At a cost of $500 to $650, a newcomer can fish a single-tip rod built by well-known rodmakers such as Jeff Wagner or A. J. Thramer. It's a great way to get started in cane.

If you are new to bamboo, sooner or later the inevitable question of "Why fish cane at all?" comes up. If you're reading this book, there is a good chance you've already made up your mind. If you haven't, I could tell you that the value of a cane rod will appreciate over the years, whereas a rod made of other materials will in all likelihood depreciate. But that's not much of a reason to fish bamboo. If you want an investment, buy real estate.

I like bamboo because each rod has a unique personality. A bamboo fly rod enhances my day on the water. I'm more able to match a rod with the kind of day I want. And most importantly, the rods have stories. There is a rodmaker somewhere who put time and thought into building the rod. And where would angling be without stories?

CHAPTER NINETEEN

The Care of Cane

March 1998. My first real mishap with a bamboo fly rod occurred several winter seasons ago in a place called Elevenmile Canyon. The South Platte River runs through it. The canyon is steep sided and can be very cold in the winter, but the river stays open because it's a tailwater. One of the great pleasures of living in Colorado is that our trout season stays open all winter and so do many of the state's tailwaters. The drawback is that it can be quite nippy.

That's the way it was on that particular late winter day. Although the sun was shining and the air temperature was probably somewhere in the 40s, it was still very cold in the shadows, where the trout happened to be very sporadically bulging to emerging midges.

For the task at hand I'd chosen the 7-foot 9-inch two-piece Delaware Special that George Maurer at Sweetwater Rods had crafted for me a number of years ago. Over the years, I've come to appreciate the rod more and more for all-purpose Rocky Mountain trout work. It's a responsive tool when the dry flies are on, but it can also handle nymph fishing with aplomb when necessary.

It was cold enough that day in Elevenmile Canyon for the line guides to gather some ice. That's not unusual at the tail end of winter in Colorado, but what I didn't pick up on was that my hands were colder than I thought. When I reached up to the tip-top guide with the thought of warming the ice a bit and then breaking it out of the guide, my half-frozen hands were simply not up to the delicacy of the operation. I snapped the tip-top off as cleanly as a razor cut to the heart. Or at least that's what it felt like when I realized I was holding the tip-top guide to my cherished cane rod in my hand and it wasn't attached to the rod anymore.

It was over that quickly, and there was nothing I could do. My rational mind told me that I would simply have to fit the now slightly shortened tip section of the rod with another tip-top guide, and it would probably cast just fine and that these things do happen. I reasoned that I'd fished cane rods for the better part of twenty years, and this was the first time I'd injured one to the point that it would be permanently altered, although clearly not unfishable. And besides, I did have another tip section and George could always make me a new tip if I needed one. In the grand scheme of things I knew everything was okay, but still, it didn't make me feel any better. It's no fun breaking a cane rod.

The facts of the matter are that I'd broken the rod in the way that most cane rods are broken. For a brief moment I'd forgotten how to care for the rod. I should have waded to the bank, put the rod down, and warmed the tip-top with my hand a bit until I could remove the ice. I shouldn't have reached up and grabbed the tip-top while bending the rod. I knew that. I just had a lapse. Very few cane rods are broken by trout. Quite a few are broken by trout fishermen.

Up until Elevenmile Canyon I'd done remarkably well in the care of cane rods department. There had been just one other incident on the Traun River in Austria where, once again, my cold hands were to blame. My grip slipped when I was taking my 8-foot Wright & McGill Granger Special down after a day's fishing. I slicked off the line guide above the ferrule almost without notice. That mishap was easily fixed and the rod, although no longer "original," still fishes as good as new.

Actually, taking care of a cane rod is not difficult or time consuming. I've come to find that they are remarkably durable. That doesn't mean that those of us who appreciate cane and those who build cane rods don't have a few quirky ideas about how they should be cared for. I think that goes with the territory. But in general there are a few hard and fast rules that everybody seems to agree on. John Gierach covers them nicely in his book, *Fishing Bamboo*, as does Martin Keane in *Classic Rods and Rodmakers*.

Everyone agrees that a bamboo rod must be dried after a day's fishing. This means that you should wipe down the rod and make sure that the cloth bag the rod goes into is dry before you store it in the aluminum case. A wet rod stored in the tube, especially for a lengthy period of time, can mildew. If that happens, it's all over.

The degree to which you must dry the rod depends to some extent on where you live. In the arid Rockies, where I live, a simple wipe of the rod after fishing may suffice, although it never hurts to dry the rod and bag overnight before storing in the tube. In damper climates care must be taken to thoroughly dry the rod and rod bag before storage.

Rod builder John Bradford, who has much experience with the restoration of rods, takes it a step further. He suggests that rods should be hung in the cloth bags when stored. Some cloth bags have a hanging loop, and for those that don't, simply attach a safety pin to the bag as a hanger. Bradford says that he hangs his rods in the back of his closet when not in use. He uses the aluminum tubes only to protect the rod when in transit to the stream.

However you choose to do it, the bottom line is that the rods must be dry when put into the tube. If the rod is going to be stored for a lengthy period of time, it probably pays to hang it outside the tube in the cloth bag or at least leave the cap off the tube.

When removing a rod from the tube, you should take the rod bag with the enclosed rod completely out of the tube. When you do this, form a ring with your thumb and forefinger over the top of the tube to protect the line guides as you slide the rod bag out. You should do the same when you return the rod to the tube.

Every rod builder agrees that the ferrules must be kept clean. Homer Jennings told me that if your rod comes with ferrule plugs for the female ferrule, be sure to use them. He also mentioned that you might want to put a thin coat of oil on the male ferrule and then wipe most of it off to prevent oxidation. He cautioned that too much oil, or any kind of lubricant, can be detrimental to ferrules because it can trap grit and grime that over time could abrade the ferrule.

John Bradford suggests coating the ferrules with a very little bit of hard beeswax (not the soft kind) to protect and lubricate the ferrule. He also recommends that if the ferrules get too tight—metal to metal—it's best to take the rod to someone who knows what they are doing or at least give them a telephone call before trying to fix it yourself.

Rod builders acknowledge that nickel silver ferrules do oxidize and that they must be cleaned at times. Opinions vary on how to clean them, but the rod builders I talked to agreed that any abrasive, however fine, should probably not be used. John Bradford suggests simply wiping the ferrules with a coarse cloth, such as a towel, a few times a year to clean them. Other rod builders say a little acetone works. The point is that if the ferrules are still tight after a basic cleaning with a coarse rag or possibly acetone, it might be time to talk with a professional before you start using any other cleaning agents.

When it comes to putting rods together and taking them down, *never* twist the ferrules. It's best to keep the hands close together when joining the ferrules. When separating ferrules, it's generally recommended that the hands be held somewhat farther apart, although I haven't strictly adhered to this rule and haven't suffered ill effects yet.

Some rods have "witness marks" on each ferrule that when lined up guarantee that the line guides will be correctly positioned. If you join a ferrule on a rod without witness marks and find that the guides are improperly aligned, pull the ferrule straight apart and start all over again. Don't be tempted to twist the ferrule, even if it's only a slight bit. If a ferrule gets stuck together, two pads of soft inner tube held in each of your rod-pulling hands will allow you to grip the rod more firmly and pull it straight apart. I've never had the inner tube ferrule pullers fail me. I always pack them when I go fishing.

In the general care and maintenance department, after each fishing trip I always make a point of inspecting a cane rod before putting it back in the rod bag after drying. Mostly what I look for are flecks in the varnish and any problems around the ferrules, line guides, wraps, or tip-top. If I find a spot where a little varnish has come off, I use a toothpick to apply a coat of thinned varnish. This will protect the cane from water marks that may occur if it's unprotected. Eventually a favorite rod will get to the point where it will need to be revarnished. The periodic inspections help me determine when to do that, and the varnish triage on the small flecks keeps the cane in shape until that time.

Although cane rods are most often broken when stepped on, closed in auto doors, or involved in other sundry idiotic mishaps, there is one common cause of breakage that occurs when they are actually engaged with a trout. It happens when a fish is being landed. The most common scenario is that the excited angler positions what he believes to be an exhausted trout at his feet, holds the rod tip straight up in the air with the butt punched into his waist, and then leans over to net the fish. The fish, which turns out to be not so exhausted, sees the net and makes a final lunge for freedom and the tip of the rod snaps. In other less severe cases the angler finds that he has indeed landed his trout, but there is a rather severe set left in the rod's tip. The fact is that when fish are landed this way the rod tip is bent over too far and damage is a real possibility.

This sort of mishap is easily prevented by extending the rod arm straight out from the body and parallel to the water while extending the net hand straight out toward the fish in the other direction. This allows the rod tip to be held in a position more horizontal to the water's surface while the fish is "led" into the net. The strain and bending on the tip are greatly lessened. If you find this classic landing pose a little too awkward to perform, you should follow John Bradford's advice. He says, "If you at least don't hold the tip straight up, you'll probably be okay."

If you do end up with a set or curve in a rod tip, for whatever reason, it can be straightened by a competent rod builder with the judicious application of heat. This isn't a project for amateurs. Take the rod to a pro.

Also included in the broken tip nightmare category is the snagged fly. If you snag a fly in a tree or on a log in the stream, don't yank and bounce the rod against the dead weight trying to unsnag the hook. It's best to lay the rod down or hand it to a companion and then grab the fly line and break off the snagged fly. It's much better to loose a fly than bust the rod tip.

It also pays to take a few precautions when walking with an assembled rod through streamside brush. Many anglers carry the rod butt section first with the rod trailing behind them. Others prefer to have the tip in front where they can keep an eye on it. I tend to carry mine butt first. However you prefer to do it, the most important thing is to take your time when navigating heavy brush.

It's also good practice to not lay the rod flat on the ground when taking a break or having lunch. Rods lying flat on the ground are hard to see and may be stepped on. Prop the rod up against a tree or brush where it can be seen and is less likely to be damaged.

When leaving your cane rod in a vehicle, it's important to keep it out of direct sunlight. Due to an increase in theft, it's also good policy to stow it out of sight. Rods should be stored away from heaters and direct sunlight at home.

Other than that, about the only thing I try to remember is to put my rod away first thing upon returning to the car after a long day of fishing. I do it before I take my waders off or think about anything else. The kiss of death is to lay a rod across the top of a vehicle and then proceed on to other chores. I know of two cane rod enthusiasts who drove off with rods left on top of their cars. Neither rod was recovered, and both anglers ended up very unhappy campers.

All in all, taking care of a cane rod is little more than common sense. If you simply remember that rods must be stored dry, ferrules must be kept clean and not be twisted, and the rod tip must not be held straight up when landing a fish, the odds are good that you will avoid the most common causes of damage to bamboo rods. Other precautions simply amount to being aware of where the rod is and keeping it out of harm's way.

It's really a small price to pay for the pleasure of fishing cane.

CHAPTER TWENTY

Fly Lines for Bamboo Rods

December 1998. Bamboo fly rod enthusiasts can talk for hours about the alchemy of cane. We verbally dissect every rod we get our hands on and rant about tapers, node staggering, action, finish, guide placement, and wraps. None of this actually has anything to do with alchemy, but you have to get the technical details out of the way before you can talk about the dreamy stuff.

When it comes to bamboo, I'm a collector only in the sense that I have a fair number of rods stacked up in the corner. I've accumulated them over the years with the intention of fishing every one of them. I like some better than others, but I seldom have the heart to sell any of them. If I do sell or trade a rod, it's only to finance the purchase of another rod that I want to fish.

That doesn't mean I have anything against collectors. It isn't difficult to make a case that handcrafted cane rods are functional art or at the very least a reasonable investment. Cane rod values go up over time; values for rods made of other materials typically go down. There will always be someone putting a rod or two away as a "hedge" against inflation. If I have any instinct at all to collect split-cane fly rods, it's because they represent an individual rod builder's life history. You can't help but think about the person who built a cane rod when you fish it. Most of the time the builder puts his name on the rod. And to me that means he's saying, "This is the best job I can do, my name's on it, and you know where to find me."

The best cane rods invariably come from the hands of builders who have gone beyond just planing and gluing bamboo together. Building fine rods is a lifestyle. Rod builders will tell you that they could make more money doing something else, but they have chosen to build rods.

I'd like to think that the reason I fish cane rods is because too much has gone into the rod to not fish it. But the truth is that I'm just too much of a hedonist to not fish them. I want to know how the rod feels when I cast it on the stream. I need to feel fish on a cane rod. I want to understand the alchemy.

With all of that in mind, I was thinking about an aspect of cane that most enthusiasts don't talk about much. It began when John Gierach sent me a 5-weight double-taper McKenzie fly line to try out. It's called the Bamboo Fly Line and has been designed and made in England especially for cane fly rods.

Most cane rod aficionados know that some fly lines are better than others for bamboo. As a rule, they look for a more supple fly line, rather than the stiff, slick "shooter" lines designed for distance when mated to a graphite rod. The name of the game, at least in lightweight and medium-weight bamboo fly rods, is delicacy of presentation and an exquisite smoothness in casting. More supple lines lend themselves to this.

The history of fishing bamboo is actually tied to fly lines. Take a look at an older cane rod—the stripper guide is often quite small in diameter. This indicates that the rod was designed for a silk fly line. These lines, which were the standard for many years, were considerably smaller in diameter than modern polyvinylchloride (PVC)-coated fly lines. They were also a pain in the neck to keep afloat and take care of. There are countless horror stories about greasing, drying, and caring for silk lines. Some historians will tell you that the silk fly line almost accounted for the demise of fly-fishing when many anglers defected to spinning tackle in the 1940s just to get away from expensive silk lines that rotted rather quickly if not properly cared for.

That changed when Leon Murtuch figured out a way to coat a braided line with a tapered PVC coating in 1952. You know the rest of the story. There are now literally hundreds of fly lines available to fly fishermen for every conceivable angling specialty. And now there's even a fly line made especially for bamboo fly rods.

It occurred to me awhile ago that the cane rod builders I have been privileged to talk to over the years do have some ideas about which modern fly lines work best on their rods. I remember John Bradford once telling me that he specifically designed a rod with the double-taper Scientific Anglers Air Cel Supreme 2 fly line in mind. He told me that other lines would work, but this particular line was the sweetest—and it had to be the ivory-colored one. The orange was too harsh for the aesthetics of the rod. I loved that part of the conversation—only a cane rod enthusiast would consider the color of a fly line.

Other rod builders mentioned other lines. The Cortland 444 consistently came up in conversation. Although double-taper lines appeared to be the favorite among rod builders and my cane rod fishing buddies for lighter-weight rods, I did run into one builder who liked the Wulff Triangle Taper for his rods.

I decided to run a test on several lines that I'd been told were good for cane rods. At first I got all jazzed about weighing lines, miking tapers, and PVC chemistry until I realized that none of the technical stuff really matters to me. I just want to know how a fly line casts. I decided to leave the science of fly lines to the techno-nerds. I would run a qualitative test, which in translation means I went down to the local park with a bag full of fly lines and cast them.

I chose 5-weight lines for the test because I tend to accumulate 5-weight cane rods. I wanted to cast them on two different 5-weight rods that represented two very different actions. I picked my South Creek 8½-foot John Gierach–A. K. Best Special Taper rod built by Mike Clark and my 7½-foot Gary Howells 3⅛-ounce rod. Both are two-piece rods. The Clark rod is a fine example of an assertive western dry fly action. The Howells is a more traditionally tapered moderate dry fly action rod.

I picked seven 5-weight lines. Five were double taper and two were weight forward designs. The two most often mentioned fly lines by cane rod builders and cane rod fly fishers were the Scientific Anglers Air Cel Supreme 2 and the Cortland 444. I also included the McKenzie Bamboo Fly Line and the Lee Wulff Triangle Taper on the recommendation of rod builders.

Bruce Richards at Scientific Anglers suggested that I try the Scientific Anglers Ultra 3 in the buckskin color. This delighted me because it meant he, too, is attuned to the color sensibilities of cane rod fishers. He also insisted that I try the Mastery XPS. Both of these lines featured Scientific Anglers new Advanced Shooting Technology (AST), which is apparently a slicker, longer-lasting version of conventional PVC coatings. Joe Wolf at Cortland recommended that I give the Cortland 444 Clear Creek a whirl.

All the lines were 30 yards in length, with the exception of the Cortland 444 Clear Creek, which is 75 feet long. Five of the lines were new right out of the box. Two of the lines were in near-new condition.

The one characteristic that all the lines had in common was that they were more supple than some stiffer lines designed for shooting on fast-action graphite rods. What I was looking for in my test was how the lines felt when cast on the different 5-weight cane rod actions and if one line would be compatible with both. I also keep track of what fly fishers call line "memory," which results in the fly line remaining coiled to varying degrees when stripped off the reel. For the purpose of the test, all lines were equipped with a 7½-foot Orvis Knotless Tapered Leader.

Here are the notes I made on each line in the order that I cast them.

Cortland Double-Taper 444. The line felt supple and retained mild to moderate memory that probably wouldn't be a factor when fishing. It cast smoothly on the Clark close-in and at moderate to longer distances. The line loaded nicely throughout a range of casting distances, and it was easy to keep the shock waves out of it. It shoots nicely. On the Howells it was a bit more difficult to keep the shock waves out of the false casts, but a little modification of the casting stroke smoothed things out. As with the Clark, the Howells rod cast the 444 nicely through a range of false casts and shoots well when called upon to do so.

Scientific Anglers Double-Taper Air Cel Supreme 2. This line feels just a little thicker to the touch than the Cortland 444. I don't know if it really is, but I like the feel. There is slightly less memory than the 444. It's a quite supple line that feels good to the touch. It can get "shocky" on the Clark if you don't watch it, but is quite smooth on the Howells. It's very similar to the Cortland 444.

Scientific Anglers Double-Taper Ultra 3. This line has less memory than the Cortland 444 or the Air Cel Supreme 2. The line feels thinner in diameter than the 444 and the Air Cel. The AST treatment gives the line an oily feel that is quite nice. It's clearly a better shooting line on the faster action Clark. It casts effortlessly with no shock waves. When cast on the Howells, it feels slightly underlined or somehow different until you get it out to about 20 feet. This makes it a bit harder to feel the rod load when casting close-in. It's a bit "shocky" on the false cast, but once again, very slight modification of the casting stroke corrects this.

Lee Wulff Triangle Taper. This is a weight forward line. The weighted section is designed to have no belly. It is tapered continuously over its length, which means that there is a delicate smaller line diameter on the business end.

The Wulff tends to overload the Clark when the majority of the weighted portion of the line is in the air. There is quite a bit of memory in the running line portion, too. Needless to say, it shoots great—it almost compels you to shoot it when the weighted portion is in the air. The line casts better than most weight forward lines on short 6- or 7-foot close-in casts. The "softer" Howells is completely overwhelmed by this line.

This line is marketed as a 5- or 6-weight, but it's clear that the 4- or 5-weight would be better on these rods.

Note: After the test I investigated the weight designations on the Wulff lines, and the manufacturer does recommend that the 4- or 5-weight be used on bamboo rods designed for 5-weight lines. So you should blame me and not the manufacturer for the overloading faux pas.

McKenzie Double-Taper Bamboo Fly Line. This line doesn't have the oily feel that most users of PVC-coated lines are familiar with. It's stickier to the touch and takes some getting used to. The texture of the line is also rougher, which is a little bit like silk lines used to be. The sandpaper-like sound of it shooting through the guides is disconcerting, although I don't know if it is actually grinding them down.

The line feels thinner in diameter in the hand and has a good bit of memory. The Clark feels underlined when cast with this line on it—maybe like a 4½-weight line rather than a 5-weight. It doesn't shoot as well as the other lines. It casts better on the more moderate action of the Howells, but once again, it may be slightly underlined. It's harder to feel the rods load with the Bamboo Fly Line.

Scientific Anglers Double-Taper Mastery Series XPS. Once again the AST coating gives this line a nice, supple oily feel. It has very little memory at all. It feels a little thicker in diameter to the touch. Casts great close-in on the Clark and throughout all casting ranges. Shoots well. The line feels good on all the tests on the Howells, too. It's among the best lines for both rods.

Cortland 444 Clear Creek. This is a weight forward line. It has the least memory of any of the lines. It feels just slightly overlined on the Clark, but it's not enough to worry about. It's good close-in and at distance. Unlike many weight forward lines, it doesn't make you feel the need to shoot when the rod is loaded any more than a double-taper line does. It does overload the Howells a little too much for my liking. The trick here may be to go down one line weight for rods with a more moderate action. If you like weight forward lines on lighter cane rods, which I don't, this is among the best I've cast.

As you can see, the test was qualitative. It was more difficult than I thought it would be, too. The bottom line is that all the lines I tested would be serviceable for use on cane rods, but you'd probably have to tinker with the line weights on some of them to get a good matchup. This is especially true for the weight forward lines. Some lines work better than others, but that may very well come down to personal taste. As I expected, the old standbys—the Cortland 444 and the Scientific Anglers Air Cel Supreme 2— appear to have a broad range of application.

These lines are good general-purpose 5-weights if you fish several rods but don't want to fine-tune each rod for a specific line. What I like about both of them is that the design has been around for a long time. The manufacturers don't seem to be messing with them. That means you may be able to depend on them to be the same over the years. There's nothing worse than finding a fly line you really like and then having it discontinued or modified by the manufacturer.

Being the old-fashioned kind of guy that I am, I don't think I really wanted to be impressed by the newer, high-tech Scientific Anglers Ultra 3 and Mastery XPS, but I have to admit I was. I liked the feel of both lines quite a bit. I hope they keep them around in their current incarnation.

One point I should make about all the lines tested is that they were new or near new. I know from experience that the Cortland 444 and the Air Cel Supreme 2 stand up well over time. I haven't fished any of the other lines long enough to see how they hold up. Needless to say, keeping any line clean will add to its life.

You'll also note that I didn't get into silk lines at all, although I know that they are being manufactured again. Silk is unique to cast, and a few cane rod enthusiasts I know are willing to put up with its eccentricities. I've also heard that the silk lines being manufactured now require less maintenance than the ones commonly used 50 or 60 years ago. The new silk lines may actually be the answer on some older cane rods, but I guess I still haven't quite developed the patience to provide whatever maintenance is now required. Having said that, I still think everyone should cast a silk line at least once in their life. Consider casting a friend's silk line first, and if you find that you can't live without one, you have my blessing. Finally, it should be noted that most cane rodmakers now take into account that modern PVC-coated fly lines will be fished on their rods.

The best way to find the ideal fly line, just like a cane rod, is to try as many different ones as you can. You may find that a particular fly line makes your rod cast better than any other line. The experience of the "perfect" fly line may compel you to develop a library of fly lines designated for specific rods. I tend more toward a general-purpose line that works well on all or most of my rods designed for a specific line weight, but I have made exceptions for rods that have unique actions.

As always, you must cast the fly lines and fish with them if at all possible. Ultimately, it comes down to personal preference. That's an important part of what the alchemy of cane is all about. When you find the line you like in the weight you like, figure that it's the one for you no matter what anyone else says. With any luck, you won't end up with a closet full of fly lines that didn't work.

May 2000. I packed a Wulff Long Belly 6-weight fly line for a short trip to fly-fish central Washington's gorgeous glacially formed lake systems and the prairie seep lakes that dot the state's eastern plains. George Maurer, the Pennsylvania rodmaker, sent the line along with the 6-weight Rocky Mountain Trout Bum rod he made for me. He wanted me to just give it a try. The translation is that George thinks the line works pretty well on his rods.

The case for the Long Belly fly line is that it combines the best features of a double-taper and a weight forward fly line. You should theoretically have the delicacy of a double-taper line close-in, but pick up some of the rod loading power of a weight forward line for longer casts. I test cast the line on George's Trout Bum and a Jim Hidy 6-weight before the trip. I couldn't really tell if the line cast as delicately as a double-taper line on the grass, but what I could tell was that I liked how it felt when cast over its entire range. The line had a nice, supple feel to it and seems to have the ability to smoothly load each of the rods over a broad range. There are no hitches where the rod suddenly acts differently because the entire weight forward portion of the taper is in the air. All in all, it seems like a good line for my heavier rods, where I'm looking for more distance but want to maintain some continuity to the feel of the rod.

After three days in a belly boat I ended up a believer in the Long Belly line. It performed well cast with an 8-foot rod from a belly boat, which is no mean feat. It is now my line of choice on both the Maurer and Hidy 6-weight rods. My tendency is to stick to double tapers for my lighter rods, but the Long Belly could be the answer for those persnickety light rods that seem to be in between a double-taper and weight forward line.

April 2001. In the world of fly-fishing mergers, Streamworks acquired McKenzie Fly Tackle Company and then 3M Scientific Anglers acquired Streamworks. That didn't leave much hope for the English-made McKenzie Bamboo Fly Line. Last word was that there were a few of the lines floating around in Oregon, but that once that supply was gone, the Bamboo Fly Line would be history.

Whether you liked the fly line or not, at least it was recognition that bamboo-phites are part of the fly-fishing population. And our numbers are growing.

CHAPTER TWENTY-ONE

Making Your Own

November 2000. Straightening a strip of bamboo doesn't seem difficult in the capable hands of master rodmaker Homer Jennings. He warms it over a heat gun and then deftly pushes, pulls, and cranks on the now pliable strip. When he thinks he's close, he holds the strip up to his eye and sights down its length. After another brief encounter with the heat gun and a few quick bends, he hands the strip to me.

"I think it's pretty good now, but you have to be on guard. It could go back a little. You usually end up having to straighten this stuff more than once," he warns.

It's my turn next. The closest I've come to building a bamboo fly rod is when I stripped, refinished, and rewrapped the line guides on garage-sale-special bamboo rods that I picked up more than a decade ago. But ever since I fell in love with the beauty and casting characteristics of split-cane fly rods twenty-five years ago, I've been edging toward building my own.

I decided to try my hand at straightening bamboo strips as a sort of preamble to the undertaking because novice and master rodmakers alike have told me that straightening the bamboo rates right near the top of the list of the most frustrating, time consuming, and more difficult of the many steps required to take six strips of bamboo from a raw state to the finished product.

Homer has thoughtfully supplied me with culled strips of bamboo for my initial attempts at straightening. The heating on the first strip goes nicely until I remove it. It snaps in two when I try to bend it.

"A little too much heat, I would say," Homer says and chuckles as I grab another strip.

I'm more careful on the next strip and manage to bend it nicely, except rather than taking the original bend out, I put a whole new bend in.

"You have to heat it right where you want it to bend. That can be the hardest part," Jennings says.

Indeed. I spend the next half hour just trying to see where a few strips need to be heated. Finally, I make a modest improvement on one bend. Jennings sights down it and says it's not too bad and then heats it a bit and straightens it perfectly.

"It takes some practice, but you do get it," he calmly says.

It's not clear when strips of bamboo were first cut and then glued together to utilize the strong, flexible "power fibers" that are found along the outside edge of a stalk, or culm, of bamboo. Some records indicate that the British may have been gluing three or four strips of bamboo together to form tips for their otherwise solid greenheart rods in the early 1800s.

In the United States it's known that Samuel Phillippe, a Pennsylvania gunsmith, split strips of bamboo, planed them to a taper, and then glued them together in 1839 to create sections for fly rods. The first rods made entirely of split cane glued together were probably three-strip rods that appeared in England around 1830. Phillippe is said to have produced four-strip rods made entirely of split bamboo by 1845.

The first six-strip split-bamboo rod made of six triangular tapered splines, which is today's standard, is generally credited to Charles Murphy of New York, but it was Hiram Leonard who brought it to the attention of American fly fishers in the 1870s. The six-strip bamboo rod gained popularity across the United states when Leonard developed a bevelling machine to make the initial cuts on the bamboo strips; this speeded production and allowed Leonard to begin turning rods out of his Maine workshop. He was also instrumental in husbanding the skills of many rodmakers whose names later became synonymous with the six-strip bamboo rod.

In the past decade or so in the United States, more and more fly fishers have humbly followed in Leonard's path by trying their hand at the exacting craft of building their own split-bamboo fly rod. Most contemporary builders hand plane the bamboo on adjustable planing forms that are not too different from the forms used in Leonard's day. While these venerable planing forms may be a bit slower than a bevelling machine, nothing beats them when it comes to making a high-quality cane fly rod. In fact, many professional rodmakers today still use only a planing form, and others use one to touch up work done with a bevelling machine.

The past five years has seen tremendous growth in books and videos on building your own cane rod, bamboo fly rod–building classes, Internet sites dedicated to building cane rods, gatherings of cane rod builders, and magazines devoted to beginning and novice cane rod builders. These days, it is probably easier for the average angler to learn about building his or her own rod—and obtain the tools and materials to do so—than ever before.

The use of planing forms is not the only aspect of modern six-strip split-bamboo fly rod making that has changed little over the years. Master rodmaker and rod-making instructor Jeff Wagner of Parma Heights, Ohio, said that there's nothing magical about making a split-cane rod. "Cane rod construction is simply forming a series of tapered cane strips and then gluing these strips together to form a blank," he said.

But while building a serviceable split-cane rod is not rocket science, it does require attention to detail in every step, precise measurements, the right tools and a basic knowledge of how to use them, and perseverance. Building a superior split-cane fly rod requires experience, craftsmanship, knowledge of materials, insight, and quite possibly a measure of grace.

Professional rodmakers such as Jennings or Wagner figure it takes anywhere from forty to sixty hours to take a raw culm of bamboo to the finished product. An accepted time frame for a novice to complete his/her first split-cane fly rod is from eighty to one hundred actual hours of work.

The basic steps in building a split-cane fly rod begin with the selection of a culm of bamboo and splitting it into strips. Subsequent steps include aligning the strips so that the nodes, or growth rings, of the bamboo are properly spaced; straightening the strips; bevelling the strips into an untapered triangular shape; heat treating the cane; planing a taper to the strips; gluing the strips together; preparing rod components such as cork grip, ferrules, and reel seat; straightening glued blanks; cutting rod sections to length; mounting ferrules, reel seat, and grip; varnishing the rod; and wrapping the line guides to the rod. Each step has its own bevy of details that must be attended to.

The universal bamboo of choice for building a split-cane fly rod is known as Tonkin cane. It is grown commercially on plantations in a limited geographic area along the Sui River in southern China. Tonkin cane is prized for its qualities of lightness, flexibility, and great strength. Fibrous vascular bundles that grow close to the outside of the hollow bamboo stalk—they're known as power fibers to rodmakers—are stronger than steel.

Typically, rodmakers purchase bamboo in bundles of twenty 12-foot-long culms. Rodmakers use the lowest 12 feet of the forty-foot tall stalks; it is in these lower sections that the walls of the bamboo are at their thickest and contain the highest concentration of power fibers. The wall consists of three layers: a hard outer layer of enamel that protects the plant, the power fibers, and an inner pithy layer. The enamel is removed during rod construction, and any woody material that is also worked away is almost always taken from the inside pithy layer of the wall, in order to remove as few of the strong outer fibers as possible.

After harvesting, while still at the plantation, the raw bamboo culms are scrubbed and then dried in the sun. Dried culms may be straightened somewhat with the application of heat before they are cut to length and bundled for shipping.

As a rule, a rodmaker purchases the twenty-culm bundles sight unseen and uses what he gets. A typical bundle contains much useable material, but all bundles have defects. Rodmakers look for straight culms that are nicely dried, with little marring caused by insects, burn marks from the straightening process, rough handling, or growers' marks burned into the enamel to identify it. Thick, dense walls containing tightly packed concentrations of power fibers are highly prized. As of this writing, a single 12-foot culm of bamboo sells anywhere from $12 to $20. A single culm will produce at least one fly rod and sometimes more. For many years Charles H. Demerest, Inc., of Bloomingdale, New Jersey, was the major importer of bamboo for rodmakers; more recently, Andy Royer at the Bamboo Broker and Tuxedo Cane have entered the importing market.

Listing the tools required to build your first split-cane fly rod is a little like detailing the tools required to tie an artificial fly. Opinions differ, but there are some basic necessities.

Planing forms. A rough wood planing form for making an untapered triangular bevel and a long (approximately 60 inches) steel final planing form to make the final tapered triangular bevel. Some rodmakers build their own planing forms, but the cost of high-quality forms is not prohibitive.

In addition, Tom Morgan, known to many cane rod aficionados from his association with the Winston Rod Company, has recently introduced a useful hand mill for rod builders. "The real advantage to the hand mill is that it uses carbide cutters and cuts two angles at once," Morgan says. "This makes it easier for beginning rod builders to use, and it's faster for anyone building a rod. The learning curve is real fast on it. It's hard to make a bad cut." Response to the hand mill has been excellent, and it has gained a following among some rodmakers.

Hand planes and blades. The Stanley model 9½ was the rodmaker's standard, but it's no longer made. The Stanley G12-020, an English reproduction, replaced it. Record Tools also makes an excellent reproduction. Rodmakers typically replace the plane blade with a high-carbon steel blade made by the Hock Blade Company. You need a #1000/#6000 combination grit water stone and honing guide to sharpen the blades.

Measuring tools. Dial indicator caliper, micrometer, and dial depth gauge for setting planing forms and measuring bamboo strips.

Saw and splitter. Japanese dovetail saw or hacksaw, for cutting bamboo strips and splines. Bamboo froe or splitting knife for splitting bamboo culms (screwdriver with a sharpened edge will work).

Binder. For binding glued splines together. Can be bought or self-made.

Oven. For drying bamboo. Can be bought or self-made.

Sanding block and sandpaper. For sanding strips and blanks.

Heat gun. For straightening bamboo strips, blanks.

Mallet and gouge. To remove nodal, or growth ring, dam from the center of split-bamboo culm.

Along with the necessary tools, rodmakers must acquire adhesives, varnish, and hardware such as ferrules, reel seat, line guides, rod wrapping silk, and grip cork.

In the past, wannabe rodmakers had difficulty in finding sources to supply the required tools, hardware, and any kind of instruction on building a split-cane rod. That began to change when *A Master's Guide to Building a Bamboo Fly Rod* by Everett Garrison with Hoagy Carmichael was published in 1977. It literally became the bible for a generation of rodmakers, many of whom are now respected full-time professional rodmakers. The book was among the first detailed step-by-step guides to what formerly had been a trade with proprietary secrets. It opened the door to the hobbyists.

Most recently a number of excellent how-to bamboo rodmaking books have been published, along with several videos. In addition, bamboo rod-making classes conducted by several well-known and respected professional rod builders have sprung up in the last few years.

Prospective first-time rodmakers are well advised to check out the possibilities of taking a rod-making class before they invest in rod-making tools and materials, which at an entry level will cost $1,500 to $2,000. Most rod-making courses last a week, and students come out of the class having built a serviceable bamboo fly rod. After you gain a working knowledge of the necessary tools and procedures, you're in a better position to determine if you really want to pursue rod making. The cost of most classes is about the same as the price of a cane rod built by a professional maker.

Rod-making instructors recommend that first-time builders select a midrange line weight such as 5 or 6 for their first rod. Recommended length is from 7 to 8 feet. A two-piece rod is best to start with.

Regardless of whether you enroll in a class or set up a workshop in the basement and go it alone, the rest comes down to blood, sweat, and tears. But I hear that once the work is done, nothing is better than catching a trout on a split-cane rod you've made yourself.

RESOURCES FOR BAMBOO RODMAKERS

Ten years ago novice bamboo rodmakers learned what they could about split cane mainly through word-of-mouth and a few classic reference texts and periodicals. That's all changed in recent years with an explosion of information on making your own split-bamboo fly rod in the form of books, periodicals devoted to cane, rod-building classes, and rod builder Internet websites.

Fly fishers interested in building their own split-cane fly rod are well advised to study and research available information before they purchase rod-building tools and supplies. Conversations with friends who have already made a rod and discussions with full-time professional rod builders can be invaluable.

Here's a partial listing of building-your-own-bamboo-fly-rod resources.

BOOKS

Barch, R. J., and Robert McKeon, comps. and eds. 1997. *Best of the Planing Form.* Hastings, MI: Alder Creek Enterprises Inc. These articles originally appeared in *The Planing Form,* a newsletter of long standing dedicated to the crafting of bamboo rods. Alder Creek Enterprises' address is 1178 Valleyview Drive, Hastings, MI 49058

Cattanach, Wayne. 1992. *Handcrafting Bamboo Fly Rods.* New York: Lyons Press. www.lyonspress.com. Phone: (212) 620-9580. This was one of the first in the new wave of interest in building your own bamboo fly rod.

Garrison, Everett, with Hoagy Carmichael. 1994. *A Master's Guide to Building a Bamboo Fly Rod.* Far Hill, NJ: Meadow Run Press. www.meadowrunpress.com. Phone: (908) 719-8858. This is a reprint of the 1977 classic. It has probably guided more of today's new generation of bamboo rodmakers than any other source.

Gould, Ray. 1999. *Constructing Cane Rods.* Portland, OR: Frank Amato Publications. www.amatobooks.com. Phone: (503) 653-8108. A step-by-step guide to makinga bamboo fly rod.

Holden, George Parker. 1999. *Idyl of the Split Bamboo.* Bedford, MA: Applewood Books. www.awb.com. Phone: (781) 271-0055. A minor classic first published in 1920.

Howell, Jack. 1998. *The Lovely Reed, an Enthusiast's Guide to Building Bamboo Fly Rods.* Boulder, CO: Pruett Publishing Company. www.gorp.com/pruett. Phone: (303) 449-4919. A step-by-step guide to making a bamboo fly rod.

Kreider, Claude. [1951] 1992. *The Bamboo Rod and How to Build it.* Grand Junction, CO: Centennial Publications. www.gorp.com/bamboo. Phone: (970) 243-8780. Details on making bamboo fly rods and other types of rods.

Maurer, George E., and Bernard P. Elser. 1998. *Fundamentals of Building a Bamboo Fly Rod.* Woodstock, VT: The Countryman Press. www.countrymanpress.com. Phone: (802) 457-4826. A step-by-step guide to making a bamboo fly rod.

PERIODICALS
The Planing Form (bimonthly). Contact Ron Barch, P.O. Box 365, Hastings, MI 49058

Power Fibers (online quarterly). www.powerfibers.com

WEBSITES
There are many more than can be listed here. Below are two Internet link pages that offer multiple listings of links for rodmakers that include information on materials, tools, and resources.

Cane Rod Links. Johnson, Gordon. http://home.teleport.com/ ~gord/cane/index.html

Jerry Foster's Rodmakers. www.canerod.com/rodmakers

BAMBOO ROD-MAKING INSTRUCTORS AND CLASSES
Cattanach, Wayne. At The Fly Factory, P.O. Box 709, Grayling, MI 49738. Phone: (989) 348-5844. E-mail: flyfactory@ troutbums.com. Website: www.troutbums.com. Cattanach was among the first rodmakers to offer a course of instruction in rod making.

Maurer, George. George Maurer's Bamboo Fly Rod Workshop. Phone: (610) 562-8595. E-mail: drbamboo@earthlink.net. Website: www.sweetwaterrods.com. Maurer is a full-time rod builder.

Wagner, J. D. 6549 Kingsdale Blvd., Parma Heights, OH 44130. Phone: (440) 845-4415. E-mail: sales@wagnerrods.com. Website: www.wagnerrods.com. Wagner is full-time rod builder.

BAMBOO SUPPLIERS

The Bamboo Broker. Andy Royer P.O. Box 491, Vashon, WA 98070. Phone: (206) 463-1273. E-mail: info@bamboo broker.com. Website: www.bamboobroker.com.

Charles H. Demarest, Inc. P.O. Box 238, Bloomingdale, NJ 07403. Phone: (973) 492-1414. E-mail: demaralon@aol.com. Website: www.tonkincane.com.

Tuxedo Cane. Phone: (209) 948 6500.

BAMBOO ROD-BUILDING TOOLS AND SUPPLIES

One of the difficulties in making your own bamboo fly rod is that tools and materials literally may come from dozens of sources. Rather than list all these sources, here are several suppliers who offer a range of tools and materials and will be able to help you locate sources for materials they do not carry.

J. D. Wagner Rodmaker. Phone: (440) 845-4415. E-mail: sales@wagnerrods.com. Website: www.wagnerrods.com.

Munro Rod Company. John Lintvet. Phone: (804) 340-1848. E-mail: jlintvet@munrorodco.com. Website: www.munro rodco.com.

Sweetwater Rods. George Maurer. Phone: (610) 562-8595. E-mail: drbamboo@earthlink.net. Website: www.sweetwaterrods.com.

Rodmaker Addresses

Carl-Johan Anderberg
Jennifer Olsson Signature Rods
P.O. Box 132
Bozeman, MT 59771
E-mail: olsson@scandiwestflyfishing.com
Website: www.scandiwestflyfishing.com

J. E. Arguello
2551 Mather Street
Brighton, CO 80601
Website: www.jearguello.com

Glenn Brackett
R. L. Winston Company
P.O. Box 411
Twin Bridges, MT 59754
E-mail: info@winstonrods.com
Website: www.winstonrods.com

John Bradford
J. A. Bradford Company
3700 Lawndale Avenue
Fort Worth, TX 76133
E-mail: jjabco@aol.com

Walt Carpenter
W. E. Carpenter Rod Co.
Box 52
Huntington Mills, PA 18622
E-mail: crpntr1@epix.net

Mike Clark
South Creek, Ltd.
415 Main Street
P.O. Box 981
Lyons, CO 80540
E-mail: southcreekltd@aol.com

Robert Gorman
Green River Rodmakers
935 Green River Road
Brattleboro. VT 05301
E-mail: robert@flyrods.com
Website: www.flyrods.com

Jim Hidy
The Hidy Rod Co.
2391 Helena View
Sebastopol, CA 95472
E-mail: Hidyrods@aol.com
Website: www.hidyrods.com

Charlie Jenkins and Steven Jenkins
C. W. Jenkins & Son, Inc.
3706 Red Bluff Lane
Glenwood Springs, CO 81601
E-mail: rodmaker@sopris.net
Website: www.jenkinsflyrods.com

H. L. Jennings
3050 Richmond Drive
Colorado Springs, CO 80922
E-mail: jenningsrod@juno.com

Ted Knott
166 Oneida Boulevard
Ancaster, Ontario L9G 3C9 Canada
E-mail: tedknott@cogeco.ca

Dwight Lyons
F. D. Lyons Rod Company
7156 S.E. 118th Drive
Portland, OR 97266
Website: www.fdlyons.com

George Maurer
Sweetwater Rods
258 Main Street
Shoemakersville, PA 19555
E-mail: drbamboo@earthlink.net
Website: www.sweetwaterrods.com

Bernard Ramanauskas
Eden Cane Ltd.
4738 51st Avenue
Edgerton, Alberta T0B 1K0 Canada
E-mail: edencane@telusplanet.net
Website: www.edencane.com

Don Schroeder
D. G. Schroeder Rod Company
3822 Brunswick Lane
Janesville, WI 53546
E-mail: schroede@inwave.com
Website: www.dgschroederrod.com

Jeff Wagner
J. D. Wagner, Inc.
6549 Kingsdale Boulevard
Parma Heights, OH 44130
E-mail: sales@wagnerrods.com
Website: www.wagnerrods.com